JESUS, RIGHT WHERE YOU WANT HIM

JESUS, RIGHT WHERE YOU WANT HIM

YOUR BIGGEST QUESTIONS.
HIS HONEST ANSWERS.

Phil Moore

MONARCH
BOOKS
Oxford, UK & Grand Rapids, Michigan, USA

Published by Monarch Books
an imprint of
Lion Hudson plc
Wilkinson House, Jordan Hill Road,
Oxford OX2 8DR, England
Email: monarch@lionhudson.com
www.lionhudson.com/monarch

ISBN 978 0 85721 677 9
e-ISBN 978 0 85721 678 6

First edition 2015

Acknowledgments
Every effort has been made to trace the original copyright holders
where required. In some cases this has proved impossible. We shall
be happy to correct any such omissions in future editions.
Scripture quotations taken from the Holy Bible, New International
Version Anglicised. Copyright © 1979, 1984, 2011 Biblica, formerly
International Bible Society. Used by permission of Hodder &
Stoughton Ltd, an Hachette UK company. All rights reserved.
"NIV" is a registered trademark of Biblica. UK trademark number
1448790.
pp. 57–58: Extract from "Billions and Billions of Demons" by
Richard Lewontin in *The New York Review of Books* copyright ©
1997, Richard Lewontin. Reprinted by permission of The New York
Review of Books and Richard Lewontin.
pp. 107–108: Extract from *Resurrection* by Géza Vermes copyright ©
2008, Géza Vermes. Reprinted by permission of Penguin Books.

A catalogue record for this book is available from the British
Library

Printed and bound in the UK, June 2015, LH26

Contents

Jesus, Right Where You Want Him

When Jeremy Paxman managed to corner the former British Home Secretary live on television, he famously refused to take no for an answer. In a brutal *Newsnight* interview that quickly went viral, the BBC presenter repeated the same question to a beleaguered Michael Howard a dozen times.

"Did you threaten to overrule him?"

"I was not entitled to instruct Derek Lewis and I did not instruct him."

"Did you threaten to overrule him?"

"The truth of the matter is that Mr Marriot was not suspended."

"Did you threaten to overrule him?"

"I did not overrule Derek Lewis."

"Did you threaten to overrule him?"

"I took advice on what I could or could not do."

"Did you threaten to overrule him, Mr Howard?"

"I did not overrule Derek Lewis."

"But did you threaten to overrule him?"

"Mr Marriot was not suspended…"

"I note you are not answering the question whether you threatened to overrule him."

"The important aspect of this, which it's very clear to bear in mind…

"I'm sorry, I'm going to be frightfully rude. It's a straight yes or no answer. Did you threaten to overrule him?"

"I gave him the benefit of my opinion in strong language."

"With respect, that is not answering the question of whether you threatened to overrule him."[1]

A lot of people imagine that Jesus of Nazareth was a bit like that – a slippery talker who mastered all of the right moves to sidestep people's toughest questions. A lot of people assume that Jesus got as tongue-tied as Michael Howard: in a corner, on the ropes and looking for an exit. But the real Jesus wasn't anything like that at all.

When we read the most reliable accounts of the life of Jesus, we discover that he was a teacher who thrived

1   Jeremy Paxman gave Michael Howard this roasting on the BBC's *Newsnight* programme on 13th May 1997.

on giving answers to people's toughest questions. Matthew and John were two of his twelve disciples, and two of the most common phrases in their eyewitness accounts of his teaching are *"Jesus answered"* and *"Jesus replied"*. They use those two phrases eighty-six times in total, because answering tough questions was one of the things that Jesus really enjoyed doing. Mark and Luke wrote two more contemporary accounts of Jesus' life and teaching, based on extensive interviews with eyewitnesses, and they also use those same two phrases sixty-nine times. All of these first-century writers tell us that Jesus constantly placed himself right where people wanted him. He gladly gave them honest answers to their toughest questions, and when they ran out of questions, he was willing to offend them in order to provoke them to ask some more. If we take the time to read the eyewitness accounts of what Jesus of Nazareth was really like, it is very surprising. He was nothing at all like Michael Howard at the hands of Jeremy Paxman.

That's why I think that you will find this short book so refreshing. I have spent my life studying the words of Jesus as recorded by his contemporaries and, in particular, I have been fascinated by his responses to our biggest questions. I have written this short book in order to give you a window into the answers given by the greatest teacher in human history to your toughest questions about life: Doesn't religion poison everything? Hasn't science freed us from the need to believe in God? How can we really trust what the Bible says? Why hasn't God put an end to all the suffering and violence and racism in our messed-up world? Why do so many Christians seem so arrogant and intolerant and homophobic? What about those passages in the Old Testament that made Richard Dawkins spit and shout so much in his book *The God Delusion*? This short book will give you Jesus' answers to all of those questions and to many more.

Jesus has put himself right where you want him. He has done so gladly. He isn't looking for the door, because he wants to meet you where your questions have placed you. Jesus is ready to give his honest answers to your biggest questions. So take a seat and ask away. As you read this book, you have Jesus right where you want him.

CHAPTER 1

Hasn't Religion Been the Cause of Appalling Violence?

It happens every single day. You see it almost every time you turn on the TV news. Somebody somewhere always seems to be doing something evil in the name of religion. Muslim terrorists are kidnapping Christian girls in northern Nigeria. Jewish soldiers are shelling Muslim Palestinians in Gaza. Islamic fighters are butchering the Christian minority in Iraq. It is therefore little wonder that one of the first questions that most people want to ask Jesus is *"Hasn't religion been the cause of appalling violence?"*

Most people expect Jesus to be put out by such a question. That's because they know so little about him. They have forgotten that he lived in an era of intense religious violence. He was its most vocal opponent and its most high-profile victim. The first time he preached at the Jewish synagogue in Nazareth, the congregation tried to kill him. When he preached at another synagogue in Galilee, the rabbis plotted how to persuade the Roman governor to crucify him. When they succeeded in their plan, the pagan soldiers who hammered nails through his hands and feet made a mockery of his claim to be the fulfilment of ancient Judaism. The crown of thorns they rammed down on his head was their response to his claim to be a greater king than Jupiter or Caesar. It therefore shouldn't surprise us when Jesus answers our first question very simply. His disarming response is *"Yes, obviously."*

I'm glad that Jesus doesn't duck our first question. Frankly, we are in dire need of his answer. We would need it even if this were a past-tense question – didn't religion cause terrible violence in the past, such as the seventh-century Arab invasion of North Africa, or the medieval Crusades, or the French Wars of Religion when the River Seine reputedly ran red with Huguenot blood? But sadly this isn't a past-tense question at all. Appalling violence in the name of religion is on the rise and it has become one of the biggest issues of our age. That's why Richard Dawkins reacts so strongly: *"It is fashionable to wax apocalyptic about the threat to humanity posed by the AIDS virus, 'mad cow' disease, and many others, but I think a case can be made that **faith** is one of the world's great evils, comparable to the smallpox virus but harder to eradicate."*[1] We need Jesus to give us his answer to this first question.

Jesus diagnosed the heart of the problem. He told the great religious thinkers of the first century that *"Isaiah was right when he prophesied about you hypocrites;*

1   Richard Dawkins said this in an article entitled "Is Science a Religion?", published in *The Humanist* magazine (January/February 1997).

as it is written: 'These people honour me with their lips, but their hearts are far from me'" (Mark 7:6). They were furious. They understood that he was telling them that the problem doesn't lie with religious faith. The problem lies with people who use religious words as a cloak to hide the evil thoughts that fill their hearts.

If we take a step back, we can see that this diagnosis makes perfect sense. When we read about the way in which the soldiers on the Fourth Crusade sacked Constantinople (a Christian city, not a Muslim one) in April 1204 AD, raping nuns and smashing church altars to pieces in order to plunder their gold, it is very difficult to believe that their true motivation was Christian piety. When we read about the way in which Catholics and Protestants planted car bombs for one another in Northern Ireland, it is hard to believe that worshipping the friend of prostitutes and lepers was ever at the forefront of their minds. There was even a joke that made the rounds during the Northern Irish Troubles. A group of men accost a stranger on the Shankill Road in Belfast and ask him, *"Which church do you go to?"* He replies, *"I don't really go to church."* They shoot back, *"We know that. But **which** church don't you go to?"* People throughout history have used religious dogma to justify their tribal conflicts. Jesus says the problem isn't religious faith. It's human hypocrisy.

If you are religious, you need to hear this. It is all too easy to react against this question by asserting that the world would be a better place if only churches were a little fuller on a Sunday. But Jesus doesn't do that.

He is not naïve. British churches were full when British soldiers used Maxim guns on the spear-wielding Zulus and Sudanese in order to extend their empire across the world. American churches were full when thousands of Africans were shipped across the Atlantic Ocean to work as slaves in the cotton fields. Christopher Hitchens has a point when he argues that *"Religion has been an enormous multiplier of tribal suspicion and hatred."*[2] When religious faith gets hijacked by our own self-centred agenda, it is toxic. People can do very evil things when they justify their actions through a false belief that they have God on their side.

Sociologists make a distinction between *superstition*, which attempts to manipulate God in order to promote our own agenda, and *religion*, which lays down our own agenda in order to serve God. I find that distinction very helpful when I consider Jesus' diagnosis of the problem. He rejects the knee-jerk reaction of Richard Dawkins or of the song where John Lennon imagines what the world would be without any heaven or any religion. We don't have to imagine. We already have a place on earth with no religion. It's called North Korea. Outlawing religion is not the solution. Jesus says that the solution isn't less religion, but more genuine religion. *"You hypocrites! Isaiah was right when he prophesied about you: 'These people honour me with their lips, but their hearts are far from me. They worship me in vain; their teachings are merely human rules'"* (Matthew 15:7–9).

2   Christopher Hitchens says this in his book *God is Not Great: How Religion Poisons Everything* (2007).

Genuine religion means *surrendering our own ambitions to God*. The symbol that has been used by Jesus' followers throughout the past two thousand years to represent his message is not the sword, the arrow or the spear. It is the cross. Genuine religion means remembering the words of Jesus when he prayed in agony in the Garden of Gethsemane the night before he was crucified: *"My Father, if it is possible, may this cup be taken from me. Yet not as I will, but as you will"* (Matthew 26:39). Religion that attempts to manipulate God to fulfil our own agenda is toxic. Religion that surrenders everything to God's agenda is heroic. Think of Francis of Assisi or Mother Teresa or William Booth and his Salvation Army. That's what they understood from the teachings of Jesus. It's what we need to understand if we want to change our increasingly violent world too.

Genuine religion means *trusting in God to set things right*. It leads to prayer, not warfare. When you hear about Islamic terrorist attacks or about rogue Christian gunmen outside American abortion clinics, it helps if you remember the way that Jesus corrected the religious leaders who opposed him: *"Are you not in error because you do not know the Scriptures or the power of God?"* (Mark 12:24). If we believe that God is weak enough for us to manipulate, it stands to reason that we will also believe he needs us to fight on his behalf. However, if we believe that God is so great that our own agenda must die, it stands to reason that we will also believe he is far too powerful to need any acts of violence on our part in order to promote his cause. Jesus taught this very firmly when a religious ethnic sect known as the Samaritans rejected him.

> *Jesus resolutely set out for Jerusalem. And he sent messengers on ahead, who went into a Samaritan village to get things ready for him; but the people there did not welcome him, because he was heading for Jerusalem. When the disciples James and John saw this, they asked, "Lord, do you want us to call fire down from heaven to destroy them?" But Jesus turned and rebuked them. Then he and his disciples went to another village. (Luke 9:51–56)*

When I first read Luke's account of this incident, I was surprised that two of Jesus' disciples would ever have thought that violence was the best way to promote God's agenda. But then I took a step back. That's precisely what happened during the Crusades: Jerusalem has fallen, so God needs his people to go to war! It's what lies behind Islamic terrorism today: the West is decadent, so God needs us to teach them a lesson. It's often what motivates homophobia or racism or religious hatred – society is changing, so God calls the faithful to rise up and fight. Jesus rebukes this strongly. He tells us to trust God to be God, without needing any help from us.

Jesus practised what he preached. When he was arrested in the Garden of Gethsemane, he forbade his followers from resisting his crucifiers: *"How then would the Scriptures be fulfilled that say it must happen in this way?"* (Matthew 26:54). When he was nailed to the cross and tormented by pagan soldiers and by Jewish rabbis, he responded with a prayer: *"Father, forgive them, for they do not know what they are doing"* (Luke 23:34). The Bible tells us that this is very significant. *"He offered up prayers and petitions with fervent cries and tears to the one who could save him from death, and he was heard because of his reverent submission"* (Hebrews 5:7).

Jesus modelled genuine religion for us, and his prayers were answered because of his reverent submission. Although he died, three days later rumours began to circulate that many people had witnessed that he was alive. The Roman soldiers and the Jewish rabbis were forced to admit that his tomb was empty and that they had no clue where his body was. Today, Jesus of Nazareth is the most famous man in history. More songs have been sung about him, more books have been inspired by him and more movies have been made about him than about anybody else, ever. Jesus has shown us what happens when we surrender our own agenda to God and stop trying to tell him what to do. He doesn't just answer our question. He personifies the answer.

You are right: superstition is toxic. But the answer isn't to eradicate religion. It is to discover genuine religion as it was taught by Jesus. That's the message our violent world so desperately needs to hear.

CHAPTER 2

Can There Ever Be a Just War?

That first answer raises a second one. If Jesus tells us that we need to trust God to set things right without resorting to violence ourselves, does that therefore mean that Jesus is a pacifist? Does Jesus tell us that there is never any circumstance under which it might be right and fitting for a nation to go to war?

Be careful not to answer this question too quickly. It has exercised the greatest minds in history, so if you find it easy to answer then it is possible you have failed to grasp the complexity of the question. Jesus does not respond with trite answers, and nor should we. We need to take the time to think and listen. Is there such a thing as a just war?

Some people leap very quickly towards the knee-jerk answer *yes*. If you are one of them, slow down a little. Consider for a moment the fact that Jesus lived in enemy-occupied territory where people were forced to carry heavy burdens for Roman soldiers and to pay heavy taxes to the Roman emperor. If there has ever been a context in which taking up arms was justified, it was first-century Israel; yet Jesus taught his followers to *"Give back to Caesar what is Caesar's"* and that *"If anyone forces you to go one mile, go with them two miles"* (Matthew 22:21 and 5:41). He told them, *"Do not resist an evil person. If anyone slaps you on the right cheek, turn to them the other cheek also. And if anyone wants to sue you and take your shirt, hand over your coat as well.... Love your enemies and pray for those who persecute you"* (Matthew 5:39–45). Before you answer a quick yes to this question, you need to be able to explain how Jesus' command to love your enemies permits you to shoot bullets at them.

Other people leap very quickly towards the knee-jerk answer *no*. They argue that all war is murder and that there can therefore be no such thing as a just war. If this is you, slow down a little too. When a Roman centurion believed that Jesus could heal his servant several miles away because he was used to responding to commands from Rome (Matthew 8:5–13), Jesus commended him for his faith without challenging him, Columbo-style, with a final question: *"Now just explain to me again this whole Roman army thing?"* When Jesus' friend John the Baptist led a group of soldiers to repentance, he gave them clear instructions about what it meant for them to adjust their lives to worship God: *"Don't extort money and don't accuse people falsely – be content with your pay"* (Luke 3:14). He told them to be honest and contented soldiers, but he didn't tell them to stop being soldiers altogether. Jesus puts himself right where we want him because we need to hear his answers. Faced with aggressive and advancing evil in the world, we cannot satisfy ourselves with over-easy statements about pacifism.

The first thing Jesus tells us is that *there are fewer just wars than most of us think*. In the previous chapter we mentioned the Crusades. One of them was launched when Bernard of Clairvaux preached in France on 31st March 1146: *"You who listen to me! Hurry to appease the anger of heaven… The din of arms, the danger, the labours, the uniform of war – these are the penances that God now requires of you. Hurry to atone for your sins through victories over the Infidels, and let the rescue of the holy places be the rewards of your repentance.… Cursed be the one who does not stain his sword with blood!"*[1] At the time, almost everybody viewed the Crusades as a just war, but with hindsight we can see clearly that they were largely wars of European expansionism. So let's not be naïve. Hindsight is a wonderful thing. None of us knows how history will judge our own generation's wars.

Jesus says that many military heroes throughout history have been those who refused to fight unjust wars. His teaching inspired the Roman legionary Martin of Tours to suffer jail time in 336 AD for refusing to attack a group of Gauls who were defending their homes. He told his commander, *"I am a soldier of*

---

1   James Meeker Ludlow in *The Age of the Crusades* (1896). In fairness to Bernard, in later life he deeply regretted preaching this sermon, displaying the same remorse as many politicians after the Second Gulf War.

Christ. I cannot fight."[2] Jesus' teaching inspired many British Christians to endure hatred for condemning Britain's Opium Wars with China and its leading role in the partition of Africa. War is always tragic, so it is only ever justified when the price of peace is more tragic still. Jesus warns us not to entertain the greedy general who demands a holy blessing upon his unholy ambition.

The second thing Jesus tells us is that *war is only justified when it comes as a last resort.* It helps if we understand that his command to turn the other cheek is addressed to individuals rather than to nations (one of his early followers explains in Romans 13:1–4 that God has entrusted national rulers with *"the sword... They are God's servants, agents of wrath to bring punishment on the wrongdoer"*), but this must not at all make us assume that he has therefore given national rulers carte blanche to go to war. When Jesus was betrayed by Judas Iscariot in the Garden of Gethsemane, one of his disciples decided to use force to defend him: *"One of Jesus' companions reached for his sword, drew it out and struck the servant of the high priest, cutting off his ear."* It was not wrong for Peter to wear a sword (Luke 22:36), but it was wrong for him to draw it too quickly. *"'Put your sword back in its place,' Jesus said to him, 'for all who draw the sword will die by the sword'"* (Matthew 26:51–53). Jesus warns that getting a sword out of its scabbard, a gun out of its holster or a warplane out of

2   The story of Martin of Tours is told by Mark Kurlansky in his book *Non-Violence: The History of a Dangerous Idea* (2006). Martin was later released and became the bishop of his French city.

its hangar can cause far more problems than it solves. We must exhaust all other options before the use of force is ever justified. Haste into battle does not push back the forces of evil in the world. It rashly multiplies them.

The third thing Jesus tells us is that *war is only justified when it has clear and measured aims*. We can see this most clearly in a famous passage in the gospels:

> When it was almost time for the Jewish Passover, Jesus went up to Jerusalem. In the temple courts he found people selling cattle, sheep and doves, and others sitting at tables exchanging money. So he made a whip out of cords, and drove all from the temple courts, both sheep and cattle; he scattered the coins of the money-changers and overturned their tables. To those who sold doves he said, "Get these out of here! Stop turning my Father's house into a market!" His disciples remembered that it is written: "Zeal for your house will consume me." (John 2:13–17)

This incident reminds us that we must not go to war out of rage. Jesus is consumed with a desire to set wrong right, yet he never loses control of his actions. He does not lash out against the traders in the Temple. He goes away and patiently fashions a corded whip before he acts. Rage entices people to fight battles they know they cannot win, but angry talk of honour never justifies military suicide. Rage provokes acts of rape and violence towards civilians and the mistreatment of prisoners, so war is never justified unless a commander is certain that he can control his troops in victory.

This incident also reminds us that we must not go

to war out of hatred and revenge. John's eyewitness account tells us that Jesus used his whip to drive out the sheep and the cattle, but it does not tell us that he whipped the tradesmen. He pushed over tables but not the money-changers. He did not see the merchants as his enemies, but as the victims of a sinful world that has lost sight of what really matters. He is not like the politicians who authorized the unnecessary incendiary bombing of Dresden while Winston Churchill was away at the Yalta Conference. He is more like Churchill when he reached out to those under Nazi rule, distancing them from their leaders with an assurance that *"Never will I believe that the soul of France is dead.... Italians, I will tell you the truth. It is all because of one man. One man and one man alone has ranged the Italian people in deadly struggle... against the wishes of the Italian people, who had no lust for this war."*[3] If we view our enemies not as demons, but as the hoodwinked victims of the Devil, we can love them even as we fight them. We can fulfil these words of Jesus even as we go to war: *"Blessed are the peacemakers, for they will be called children of God"* (Matthew 5:9).

Jesus has put himself right where we want him. He has answered our second question. But where does this mean he wants us to put ourselves? Does he support us if we wish to sign up for the armed services? Yes, but with one big proviso. We should only enlist if we are convinced that our government will only ever

3   Winston Churchill said this to the French and Italians in his radio broadcasts on 21st October and 23rd December 1940.

send us into battles that will make the world better, never worse. If we are convinced of this, we can serve well, knowing that *"Greater love has no one than this: to lay down one's life for one's friends"* (John 15:13). If we are unconvinced, we must not commit ourselves to serving two conflicting masters.

Even if you have no desire to join the armed services, Jesus still wants his answer to challenge you. He doesn't want you to be either an armchair critic or an armchair admirer. He calls you to enlist in his great fight against all of the evil in the world: *"Do not suppose that I have come to bring peace to the earth. I did not come to bring peace, but a sword"* (Matthew 10:34). Jesus calls you to open your eyes to the evil that advances all around you. He calls you to pick sides and he offers to teach you how to wield his weapons of love, justice and mercy. Will you fight alongside Jesus on the battlefield of this troubled world? Will you fight with him against sin and injustice? Will you fight for all that is good in the world?

Make no mistake. There is a war on, and Jesus is recruiting an army of soldiers. He came into this world to make it better, and he asks you to fight by his side.

CHAPTER 3

How Can a Loving God Allow So Much Suffering?

I have lots of friends who are unlike me, but I have one friend who is just the same as me. Kevin is tall and loud like me. He is the same age as me. He has a similar-sized family to me. He likes the same sports as me. He has the same job as me. When he was in London recently, he stayed at my house for a week. It was freaky how much we had in common.

Two weeks after he returned home, his favourite team were playing football, so he left work early and travelled home on his scooter to watch the big game. At an intersection close to his home, he was struck by a hit-and-run driver who sped through the red lights and sent him flying through the air. He never got to watch the big game. He landed on his head and suffered brain damage, which, at this stage at least, appears to be permanent. He can no longer talk. He can no longer walk. He can no longer live with his family. I feel like crying even as I write about it now. I have lost count of the number of times in the past few months that I have prayed for him and found myself asking the same burning question: How can a loving God allow such senseless suffering?

You must have asked this same question yourself. Whenever I talk with friends outside the Church, it is one of the biggest reasons they give for why they could never see themselves following Jesus. Whenever I talk with my Church friends, if they are honest, they say it is one of the biggest questions that lurks under the surface of their walk with God too. Just this last week, two of my good friends miscarried yet again. Why does God let so many bad things happen to so many good people?

I'm glad that we have Jesus right where we want him. Questions such as this one make me very grateful to Matthew, Mark, Luke and John for giving us a record of his lifestyle and his teaching. Jesus doesn't try to duck his way out of this question. He answers it by getting down in the dirt with lepers, prostitutes, beggars, no-hopers and anybody else who is in intense suffering. He begins his public ministry by announcing in Luke 4 that *"The Spirit of the Sovereign Lord is on me, because the Lord has anointed me to proclaim good news to the poor. He has sent me to bind up the broken-hearted, to proclaim freedom for the captives and release from darkness for the prisoners… to comfort all who mourn, and provide for those who grieve."* These are the first few verses of an ancient prophecy that spoke of God's desire to help those who are confused and in pain. It tells us that *"In all their distress he too was distressed."*[1]

1   Isaiah 61:1–3 and 63:9. These words were prophesied 700 years before the birth of Jesus.

I have been following Jesus for over twenty years now. My confusion over what is happening to Kevin is painful, but it is nothing new. Over these two decades I have found that Jesus answers this question in three big ways throughout the gospels. None of them is purely academic. Kevin's wife and children don't need a theological treatise. Their questions are intensely personal. That's why Jesus' answers all focus on the fact that he has walked in our shoes.

First, *Jesus reminds us of his own suffering.* Earlier this year, I experienced a sudden bereavement. I was devastated and for several weeks my mind kept returning to anguished prayer whenever I was alone. One particular evening, my distress became so severe that I cried out, *"Jesus, I'm in agony. This is a terrible cross you are asking me to bear."* The moment that I said it I felt like a fool. Who am I to talk to Jesus about bearing crosses? Mine are metaphors, but his was real and wooden and rough and bloodstained. Jesus does not try to comfort us with abstract philosophy. He offers us something far more valuable. He reminds us that he has suffered far more than any of us and he offers to carry us through our own moments of pain.

Jesus was the inconvenient baby of Bethlehem, born in a cowshed and laid in a feeding trough because there was no room at the inn for him. Before he was old enough to walk, he became a fugitive and an asylum seeker, hiding in Egypt from the murder plots of King Herod back home. As a child he was despised by his neighbours who considered talk about a virgin birth

27

to be a barefaced lie. His father died, making him the chief breadwinner for his family. In his twenties, Jesus became virtually the only single man left in his village. In a culture that prized family and childrearing, he was forced to watch as all of his childhood friends became husbands and wives and fathers and mothers, while he remained alone. In his thirties, he was hated and threatened and betrayed and whipped and crucified. We cannot shake our fists at God as if he merely issued edicts from the comfort of heaven. He has experienced this world's suffering at first hand. Whenever we are tempted to shout out this question to God, it helps if we remember that Jesus has already embraced it, quite literally, with open arms.

Second, *Jesus reminds us of God's wisdom*. A couple of nights before my final exams at university, my girlfriend broke up with me. I wish that I could tell you that I took it like a man but, in reality, I threw a tantrum at God like a baby. I lay on my bed and I pounded it with my fists. Call yourself a good God? Then what is this? And the timing, just before my finals? Is that meant to be some kind of joke? It's a bit embarrassing to admit how much I cried and shouted at the ceiling, but I want to be real with you because here's the thing: today I look back on that break-up and I thank the Lord for his amazing wisdom. Had I not been single for the few years that followed, I would have missed out on some of the most exciting adventures of my life. I would have remained stuck in a relationship that wasn't healthy, and I would not have met and married

28

my wife. I would not have my four children. Looking back, I regularly praise God for what I treated at the time as an act of his terrible cruelty.

I find that thought hugely challenging. If the benefit of a few years' hindsight enables me to praise God for traumas in the past, how much more will I praise God when I finally discover the full picture of his wisdom at the end of time? It will be like watching a street performer painting a chaotic picture to confuse the crowds, before suddenly flipping it over to reveal a beautiful picture which the crowds failed to see because their perspective was all wrong. Jesus endured the cross because he trusted in his Father's wisdom and ability to transform even the torture of crucifixion into something beautiful and good. He encourages us to trust in God's wisdom too, believing that a day is coming when the picture of our lives will finally be turned the right way up and when our mouths will be filled with gasps of worship instead of groaning and despair. Our biggest questions in this world will not remain our biggest questions when Jesus is revealed in all his glory on that Final Day.

That's why, thirdly, *Jesus reminds us to keep an eternal perspective*. John's eyewitness account particularly focuses on the internal life of Jesus – his thoughts, his motives and the way in which he viewed the world. John explains that Jesus was willing to do the work of a household slave, washing his disciples' dirty feet because he *"knew that the Father had put all things under his power, and that he had come from God and was returning to God"* (John 13:3). We live in a culture that prizes the here-and-now and reacts angrily whenever God dares to infringe upon our right to enjoy an endless stream of trouble-free days. Jesus was willing to wash his disciples' feet – even those of Judas the betrayer – because he rejected that blinkered here-and-now perspective. He viewed the world with heaven's eternal perspective and it changed everything for him. Knowing where he had come from and where he was going inspired him to endure temporary hardships for the sake of long-term gain. Even though it cost him dearly at the time in terms of pain and suffering and loss, he believed it was all part of God's perfect plan, which would echo throughout eternity.

Spending time with Jesus and listening to these three answers has changed my life. The more I grasp of his distress, the more I find that I can bear my own pain and confusion. The more I reflect on the fact that the most painful moment of his life was also his most triumphant moment, the more I find that I am able to trust in God's perfect wisdom, even though I only grasp a little of it in the here-and-now. Today we call the day on which Jesus died *Good* Friday. The Red Cross was named for the fact that his sacrifice brings hope to a hurting world. This thought helps me whenever suffering punctures my safe world. I am learning to treat it as the window through which God's true perspective on my life begins to shine. That's why Jesus encouraged his followers:

Blessed are you who are poor, for yours is the kingdom of God. Blessed are you who hunger now, for you will be satisfied. Blessed are you who weep now, for you will laugh.... But woe to you who are rich, for you have already received your comfort. Woe to you who are well fed now, for you will go hungry. Woe to you who laugh now, for you will mourn and weep. (Luke 6:20–21, 24–25)

Jesus put himself right where we needed him when he died on the cross. He is uniquely placed to help us when injustice and suffering make us cry out that God ought to help us. He shows us his own nail-scarred hands and reassures us: God already has. As he continues to answer our questions, Jesus is about to explain to us how.

CHAPTER 4

Is It Wrong to Feel Angry Towards God?

In the TV series *The West Wing*, President Bartlet orders his security detail to clear Washington DC's National Cathedral so that he can vent his anger towards God. His secretary has just been killed in her brand new car by a drunk driver, and his protégé, Josh Lyman, has been shot and almost killed.

> *You're a son of a bitch, you know that? She bought her first new car and you hit her with a drunk driver. What, was that supposed to be funny? "You can't conceive, nor can I, the appalling strangeness of the mercy of God," says Graham Greene. I don't know whose ass he was kissing there because I think you're just vindictive. What was Josh Lyman? A warning shot? That was my son. What did I ever do to yours except praise his glory and praise his name?*[1]

1   *The West Wing*, season 2, episode 22 – "Two Cathedrals" (2001).

So here's the question: Is President Bartlet wrong to pray to God this way? Is he wrong to voice such angry feelings? The reason I am asking this is that many people feel precisely the same way. When they read a book like this one, it stokes their anger towards a God whom they believe has let them down. Once again, Jesus makes no attempt to dodge our question. He is very glad we asked.

Jesus answers this question as much through his example as through his teaching. He has modelled for us how we ought to act in the darkest moments of our lives. He is honest with his disciples in the Garden of Gethsemane: *"My soul is overwhelmed with sorrow to the point of death"* (Matthew 26:38). He is so weighed down by the stress of his impending crucifixion that the capillaries in his forehead burst under the strain and *"his sweat was like drops of blood falling to the ground"* (Luke 22:44).[2] How did Jesus handle such intense feelings? Did he bottle them up? Did he fake it with God? *"Being in anguish, he prayed more earnestly"* (Luke 22:44). He turned his inner torment into prayers in which he was honest with his Father about the pain and confusion he was feeling. *"My God, my God, why have you forsaken me?"* (Matthew 27:46).

If you know the Bible well, you will recognize that last prayer as a quotation from the first line of Psalm 22. I find that very interesting, because I am frequently

2   Known as hematidrosis, this medical condition only occurs in rare cases of exceptional stress. It was recorded among a handful of soldiers in the trenches of World War One.

shocked by the language the psalmists used when they prayed. One of the most shocking psalmists is a man named Asaph, who accuses God of failing the entire nation of Israel: *"Why have you rejected us for ever, O God?... Why do you hold back your hand?"* (Psalm 74). Even more surprising than Asaph's language is the fact that Jesus actually commends him by quoting from his psalms and telling his disciples that we have much to learn from Asaph as a prophet (Matthew 13:34–35). If we feel angry towards God, Jesus encourages us to tell him so. The Lord hates fake faith and pretend praise, but he loves it whenever we are honest with him about how we really feel.

Jesus doesn't stop there. This is only half the picture. Jesus did not vent his feelings in prayer for its own sake. He was honest with his Father because he knew it was the only way for their relationship to grow stronger. It was only after he confessed to feeling abandoned that he was able to declare in faith, *"Father, into your hands I commit my spirit"* (Luke 23:46). In the same way, it was only after Asaph confessed his anger and confusion that he found peace: *"When I tried to understand all this, it troubled me deeply till I entered the sanctuary of God; then I understood... It is good to be near God. I have made the Sovereign Lord my refuge"* (Psalm 73). Honest prayer achieves far more than simply the expression of our emotions. It is like putting our heart on the operating table and asking God to heal it. Being honest with God transforms our feelings even as we pray.

This is such an important lesson for us to learn that an entire chapter in the gospels illustrates it in very practical terms. It may help you to read John 11 before you continue. God wants to help you process your own feelings as you read.

John 11 begins with Jesus appearing to fail his followers. He receives a message from Mary and Martha that tells him that his good friend Lazarus has contracted a fatal illness. Jesus responds with an amazing promise: *"This sickness will not end in death. No, it is for God's glory so that God's Son may be glorified through it."* He stays where he is for two more days but then suddenly fresh news comes through. Lazarus has died. It looks as though Jesus has lied and failed his friends precisely when they needed him the most.

John records this incident in quite some detail for two reasons. First, he was one of the twelve disciples and was close friends with Lazarus, so he experienced this personally. Second, he knows that we will experience many incidents like this one and he wants to teach us how to process our own disappointments and anger towards God.

In the original Greek text of his gospel, John tells us literally that *"Jesus loved Martha and her sister and Lazarus. **Therefore** when he heard that Lazarus was ill, he stayed where he was two more days."* Therefore? How can that be an expression of God's love? John wants us to grasp that delays and disappointments never mean that God has let us down. They are often a sign that he loves us and has something new to teach us. He

35

doesn't want our faith to be like that of Julie Andrews's character in *The Sound of Music*, closing our eyes to the storm as we sing about a few of our favourite things. Instead, he wants to develop in us a robust faith that can face up to the full force of life's frequent storms.

Jesus breaks the news to the disciples in a shocking fashion. He tells them that *"Lazarus is dead, and for your sake **I am glad I was not there**, so that you may believe."* How can Jesus say that he is glad to have put his friends through such bereavement? Because faith is like a muscle and disappointments are the gym in which that muscle grows. Like a loving father, God takes a long-term view and is always willing to put us through some short-term pain in order to grow us into better men and women. He is prepared to endure our anger because he knows that it is often the only way to open our eyes to the greatness of his purposes and his power.

One of the twelve disciples has gone down in history as Doubting Thomas. I find it interesting that Jesus still chose him in spite of his angry cynicism. Thomas makes no attempt to hide his disappointment or his conviction that heading south is far more likely to result in Jesus dying than it is in Lazarus being raised from the dead. *"Let us also go, that we may die with him,"* he says with all the positivity of Eeyore in one of A. A. Milne's *Winnie-the-Pooh* stories. Jesus does not rebuke Thomas for his anger. He is pleased, because such honesty is needed if we are to find real faith in him.

When Jesus finally arrives at Mary and Martha's hometown, their brother Lazarus has been dead for four days. Mary is furious and accuses Jesus of failing her: *"Lord, if you had been here, my brother would not have died."* Jesus accepts her anger without complaining and, sure enough, it leads to breakthrough for her sister. Martha hurls the same accusation at Jesus, but her honesty leads to fumbling faith: *"Lord, if you had been here, my brother would not have died. But I know that even now God will give you whatever you ask."* When Jesus promises to raise her brother from the dead, Martha is so angry that she dismisses it as a vague promise for the future, so Jesus restates it and asks her firmly, *"Do you believe this?"* Now comes the moment of breakthrough. *"'Yes, Lord,' she replied, 'I believe that you are the Messiah, the Son of God, who is to come into the world.'"*

Mary and Martha's honesty results in real faith in Jesus. Their emotion also stirs strong emotion in Jesus. He starts weeping and, in verses 33 and 38, John uses the strange Greek word *embrimaomai* to tell us literally that Jesus *snorted like a warhorse* that is eager to charge into battle. Their anger makes Jesus angry too. He leaps into action and confronts evil by commanding at the entrance of the tomb, *"Lazarus, come out!"* Instantly, the man is made alive again. Jesus turns to the crowd and states the major lesson of the chapter: *"Did I not tell you that if you believe, you will see the glory of God?"*

If you are reading this book as a Christian, be sure to understand this lesson. If God appears to have failed you, trust that you have not yet reached the end of the story. God wants you to express your anger and confusion to him in prayer so that he can strengthen your faith muscle to show you far more of his glory. The worship leader Tim Hughes reminds us that *"Expressing anger and pain to God is a beautiful and intimate act.... In our everyday lives, the people that we are most likely to share our deepest fears and hurts with are those we love and trust the most. True intimacy can be experienced when we choose to share honestly and vulnerably."*[3] Be honest with God about your anger. Let it draw you closer to him in prayer instead of driving you away from him in bitterness.

If you are reading this book as a sceptic or a nonbeliever, be sure to understand this lesson too. Vent your anger like President Bartlet, but then do more than that. Tell God that in spite of everything, you still want to believe. Tell him that you accept the promise that Jesus made outside the tomb of Lazarus – that seeing is not believing; believing is seeing. Tell God that you want to believe, in spite of all your angry questions, and that you want him to treat your honesty in prayer as an act of faith that he will answer. Tell him that you are being honest because you want to develop robust faith in him. Tell him that you want to see and experience the glorious power of God.

---

3   Tim Hughes in *Holding Nothing Back: Embracing the Mystery of God* (2007).

CHAPTER 5

Aren't Christians a Bunch of Hypocrites?

In the animated movie *The Road to El Dorado*, two Spanish explorers played by Kevin Kline and Kenneth Branagh discover the famous city of gold, hidden deep in the jungles of South America. When they manage to convince the gullible natives to worship them as gods, the tribal chief issues a command to his men: *"Big smile – like you mean it!"*[1]

Let's face it. A lot of Christians haven't truly understood Jesus' answer to our question in the last chapter. They treat the Christian life as if it were an invitation to follow the chief's command in *The Road to El Dorado*. Whenever they are angry or upset or confused or downright sinful, they pretend they aren't. They assume that God wants them to bury their feelings away and to behave like they are shiny, happy people. But that isn't what Jesus says God wants from his followers at all. Jesus uses a strong word to describe a person who feels one thing and pretends to feel another. He calls them a *hypocrite*.

1   *The Road to El Dorado* (DreamWorks, 2000).

For many, the hypocrisy is well-meaning. Their pretence is like that of a mother or father who puts a brave face on things for the sake of their children. They act as though they are doing better than they truly are because they mistakenly believe it is the best way to encourage those around them. Their pretence is well-meaning, but it is still hypocrisy and Jesus still reacts against it strongly.

Even more toxic is the hypocrisy that is much more of a deliberate, barefaced lie. Think about the paedophile priest, the white-suited evangelist who preaches hatred towards gay men while secretly sleeping with his secretary, or the person in your team at work who claims to be a Christian but who is the laziest and loudest complainer in the office. We can all identify with Mahatma Gandhi's frustrated reply to a British missionary: *"I don't reject Christ. I love Christ. It's just that so many of you Christians are so unlike Christ. If Christians would really live according to the teachings of Christ, as found in the Bible, all of India would be Christian today."*

So what does Jesus say in response to our question? When we read his words in Matthew 23, it comes as a relief to find that he hates hypocrisy even more than we do. He uses the word *hypocrite* seven times in this one chapter alone. It comes from the Greek word *hupokritēs*, which was used in first-century theatres to describe stage actors who wore several different masks to act out several different roles within a play. Jesus therefore tells the Pharisees, the greatest

40

religious leaders of the day, that God has seen through their playacting and is about to judge them for their sin: *"Woe to you, teachers of the law and Pharisees, you hypocrites! You are like whitewashed tombs, which look beautiful on the outside but on the inside are full of the bones of the dead and everything unclean."*

These are strong words because God is rightly angered by people who are good at telling others what to do but very poor at doing it themselves. God is never fooled by our hypocrisy. Jesus is referring back to an ancient prophecy in Isaiah 5:8–30 when he curses the Pharisees seven times in this chapter with the words, *"Woe to you!"* Those are the words the Lord spoke over the religious hypocrites of Jerusalem before their city fell to the Babylonian army in 586 BC. Jesus is warning the Pharisees that God can spot a false believer a mile away.

But there is also a far more chilling side to Jesus' attack on the Pharisees in Matthew 23. It warns us that the problem of hypocrisy within the Church is not confined to a group of false believers who have infiltrated its ranks. Hypocrisy spreads throughout the Church whenever Christians forget that their salvation depends from start to finish on divine intervention and never on their own religious self-improvement plan.

Jesus warns us that we become hypocrites whenever we try to impress God in our own strength. When the Pharisees relied upon their oaths to God, their generous charitable giving, their religious rituals and their manner of honouring the ancient prophets, they were guilty of rank hypocrisy. Doing those commendable things could never make them right with God. That's one of the reasons why God sent Jesus into the world – to show us just how different a perfect, sinless human being looks from us. Hypocrisy is not just pretending to be good when we are actually evil. It is also pretending to be good enough to please God when he actually considers us to be sinners.

Many Christians are more similar to Pharisees than most of us would like to believe. Whenever people believe that their churchgoing, their Bible reading, their prayers and their charitable giving have earned them God's approval, Jesus still speaks *"Woe to you!"* over their smug sense of superiority. But it isn't just Christians who have this problem. It is just as widespread among nonbelievers who believe that when they die – in the words of one of my friends – *"I'll say, 'Look, God, I did my best and there were plenty worse than me.'"* Hypocrisy is not confined to Christians. It is a universal problem. No matter how low we set our moral standards, we always fail to meet them. If we deny this then we are worse than foolish. We are as much deluded hypocrites as any of the first-century Pharisees.

Jesus has been willing to answer our question. What remains to be seen is whether we are willing to listen to his answer. The Pharisees refused to listen and silenced him with murder, so don't act like them by giving up at this point and by throwing this short book away. Jesus holds the only remedy for hypocrisy in his nail-pierced hands. If you are willing to take it, he promises you that it will change your life forever.

First, Jesus commands us to *confess that we are sinners*. We must face up to the great gulf that exists between the people we pretend to be on the outside and the people that we truly are on the inside. We need to face up to ourselves at our very worst. Jesus warns us in verse 12 that *"Those who exalt themselves will be humbled, and those who humble themselves will be exalted."* He warns us that we can only be set free from our hypocrisy by ripping off the mask of respectability and by facing up to who we truly are.

Next, Jesus commands us to *confess that justice demands that God punish our sinfulness*. This is a bitter pill to swallow – we'll devote a whole chapter to it later on – but we have to swallow it if we are ever truly to become the people we pretend to be. When the Pharisees hesitate, Jesus shocks them in verse 33: *"You snakes! You brood of vipers! How will you escape being condemned to hell?"* There is nothing more hypocritical than denying that we have committed any sins that deserve God's judgment unless we confess them to him. Jesus invites us to step into the light so that our sins can be forgiven.

Next, Jesus commands us to *believe that his death on the cross is the only way that we can be forgiven*. Although Jesus has talked a lot about his crucifixion so far in response to our questions, he has not yet explained precisely why he died. As he predicts his crucifixion in verse 34, he reminds us of his explanation a few days earlier: *"The Son of Man did not come to be served, but to serve, and to give his life as a ransom for many"* (Matthew 20:28). People in the first century used the word "ransom" to describe the gift a convicted criminal's family was permitted to pay to the victim's family so that their guilty loved one could be spared death row and set free. Jesus died on the cross so that his blood could pay this ransom price for your sin and for mine. The only innocent person who has ever lived was nailed to a cross so that he could take the punishment for every guilty person who has ever lived. We can only access God's forgiveness if we admit that we are in desperate need of it. Christian faith always begins with the admission that we are sinners who need the crucified Jesus to pay our ransom price and save us.

Finally, Jesus commands us to *continue in the same way that we started*. Confessing our sins is not a one-off event. We do not graduate from a single moment of honesty into a lifetime of renewed hypocrisy. Being a Christian means admitting that you still struggle with sin, that areas of your life are still in a mess, and that many nonbelievers still act more kindly and more lovingly than you. It means confessing daily that your hope still lies entirely in Jesus' perfection and never in your own. Whenever Christians forget this, their religious self-congratulation is rightfully repulsive. Jesus points out in Matthew 23:13 that they *"shut the door of the kingdom of heaven in people's faces."* But whenever Christians remember that they are sinners saved by God's daily grace, their humble authenticity is wonderfully attractive. Whenever churches stop pretending that they are perfect communities and start confessing that they are merely sinful communities with a perfect Saviour, they always become places where Jesus loves to reveal himself in power.

Whenever churches remember this, they place Jesus right where people need him. They provoke people to consider: If Jesus was willing to die for sinful people like this lot, then maybe – just maybe – he was also willing to die for a sinner like me.

The fact that the Church is full of sinners shouldn't surprise us. It should encourage us. It means that God wants to save ordinary people, like you and me. It means that there is always room for one more sinner to step inside.

CHAPTER 6

Isn't the Bible Full of Myths and Contradictions?

In 2004, the American magician Penn Jillette presented a TV show entitled *The Bible: Fact or Fiction?* Already an outspoken atheist, his conclusion wasn't surprising but it was brutal: *"It's fair to say that the Bible contains equal amounts of fact, history, and pizza."*

In 2010, the British atheist Richard Dawkins agreed. In a debate about the right curriculum to teach in schools, he expressed his view that *"The Bible should be taught, but emphatically not as reality. It is fiction, myth, poetry, anything but reality."*

We need to ask Jesus to respond to such strong opinions. In the first five chapters of this book we have studied the words of the gospel writers in the Bible, but how reliable are those words? Are Penn Jillette and Richard Dawkins being fair when they dismiss the Christian Scriptures as a collection of contradictory myths and fables?

When we ask Jesus this question, his answer is very surprising. You see, Jesus lived in a culture where many people doubted, despised and denied large sections of the Bible. We tend to forget this, snobbishly assuming that freethinking is exclusively a twenty-first-century phenomenon. But it isn't. Far from it. The first century was just as cynical an age as our own. Doubting Thomas earned his name because first-century Jews often doubted. Diogenes the Cynic earned his name because ancient Greeks and Romans often doubted too. Jesus was surrounded by *Roman relativists*, people like Pontius Pilate, who dismissed God's Word with a peremptory sneer: *"What is truth?"* (John 18:38). Jesus was surrounded by *Pharisee moralists*, who found plenty of reasons to ignore the many Bible passages that speak about God's love and forgiveness towards sinners. Jesus was surrounded by *Sadducee materialists*, who rejected any Bible passage that talked about miracles which could not be explained away through scientific reasoning. Jesus lived in a culture much like ours, so he frequently answered this question. But his response was very different from the one we might have expected him to give.

I would have expected Jesus to reply, *"Which contradictions? Show me one."* I would have expected him to tackle the biggest flaw in the argument that the Bible is full of contradictory myths – the lack of concrete examples to back up the claim. Richard Dawkins mainly speaks in generalities, and Penn Jillette chose to make his TV programme using a voiceover instead of debating face to face with leading biblical scholars. I would have expected Jesus to demand specific examples and then to point out that there are three robust explanations for what are labelled contradictions in the Bible.

Sometimes there are *copyist errors*. Before the invention of the printing press, hardworking scribes were forced to make copies of the Scriptures by hand. When 2 Kings 8:26 tells us that Ahaziah became king of Judah at the age of twenty-two and some translations of 2 Chronicles 22:2 says he was forty-two, it simply means that a scribe miscopied the text of 2 Chronicles 22:2. But this is not how Jesus answers the question.

Sometimes supposed contradictions are revealed on closer inspection to be nothing more than *complementary perspectives*. The statements "Cristiano Ronaldo plays for Real Madrid" and "Cristiano Ronaldo does not play for Real Madrid" are contradictory. The statements "Cristiano Ronaldo plays for Real Madrid" and "Cristiano Ronaldo plays for Portugal" are not. In the same way, when 2 Samuel 24:1 and 1 Chronicles 21:1 tell us that both God and the Devil stirred King David to take up a census of Israel, we are meant to see it as a statement that the Devil is only permitted to act if his schemes fit within God's overarching plan. When John says that a group of women set off to visit Jesus' tomb *"while it was still dark"*, and Matthew and Mark say that the women set off *"at dawn"* and arrived *"just after sunrise"*, they are simply recording the discovery of the empty tomb from three complementary perspectives. But Jesus doesn't answer our question this way either.

Sometimes supposed contradictions are the result of *our incomplete historical knowledge*. Nineteenth-century scholars used to rubbish the miracle described in John 5 because there was no evidence of there ever having been a pool in Jerusalem with five covered colonnades – that is, until 1888 when archaeologists unearthed the remains of a pool exactly as John had described it. Modern historians used to dismiss the Bible stories about King David because they lacked archaeological evidence to corroborate his reign – that is until 1993, when new discoveries forced them to revise their former scepticism. Did the reign of David suddenly transform from myth into history in 1993, or is it simply that up until that moment modern historians were making snap judgments based upon their incomplete knowledge of the period?

I personally find these three responses very convincing, which is why I am so surprised that Jesus did not use any of them when he answered this question. He told the Romans, Pharisees and Sadducees that their question was not an intellectual one that had arisen from their heads, but a moral one that had arisen from their stubborn and rebellious hearts. Jesus warned them that their doubts were not due to the Bible being incoherent. They were due to the message of the Bible being downright inconvenient.

For this reason, Jesus refused to answer the Roman relativists on their own terms. When Pontius Pilate waved away the Scriptures with the flippant question *"What is truth?"*, Jesus responded by allowing the

Roman governor to crucify him because *"How else would the Scriptures be fulfilled?"* (Matthew 26:54). He treated Pilate's cynicism as a rehash of the age-old question the Snake had asked in the Garden of Eden: *"Did God really say?"* (Genesis 3:1). Jesus had already responded to this question by answering the Devil three times during his temptations with the statement *"It is written"* (Matthew 4:1–11). He therefore made it clear that Pilate's problem was not that the Bible's words were self-contradictory, but that the Bible's words contradicted his determination to do wrong.

Hugh Hefner, the founder of *Playboy* magazine, typifies the same moral relativism in our own day: *"It's perfectly clear to me that religion is a myth. It's something we have invented to explain the inexplicable.... I think anyone who suggests that they have the answer is motivated by the need to invent answers, because we have no such answers."*[1] King Herod out-Hugh-Hefnered Hugh Hefner. He divorced his wife in order to run off with his sister-in-law and, having done so, he forced his teenaged stepdaughter to dance seductively for him and his friends because she had a better body than her mother. Jesus did not respond to Herod's actions by debating the truthfulness of Scripture. He simply warned him, *"Haven't you read that at the beginning the Creator 'made them male and female,' and said, 'For this reason a man will leave his father and mother and be united to his wife'?... Therefore what God has joined together, let no one separate"* (Matthew 19:4–6). Jesus saw Herod's

1   Hugh Hefner in an interview with *Playboy* magazine (January 2000).

doubt as a smokescreen for defiance and his cynicism as an excuse for sin.

Jesus also refused to answer the moralistic Pharisees on their own terms. He never defended the Scripture verses they rejected for portraying God as too loving, too merciful and too forgiving towards sinners. He simply restated those verses and warned the Pharisees that *"Scripture cannot be broken"* (John 10:35) – in other words, if we have a problem with a Bible passage then it is evidence of a problem within us. It is our hearts that are broken, not the Bible. Jesus warned the Pharisees that their downplaying of certain Scriptures was simply proof that their hearts were stubborn. *"You study the Scriptures... yet **you refuse to come to me** to have life"* (John 5:39–40). *"Go and learn what this means [in Hosea 6:6]: 'I desire mercy, not sacrifice.'... If you had known what these words mean, 'I desire mercy, not sacrifice,' you would not have condemned the innocent"* (Matthew 9:13 and 12:7).

In the same way, Jesus refused to answer the materialistic Sadducees on their own terms. They came to him with what they thought was a killer question, proving beyond doubt that the Bible is full of myths: "If people will truly be raised from the dead at the end of time, then to whom will a woman widowed seven times be married?" Jesus told them that their question had revealed a problem in their own hearts, not in the Bible. It proved how little they understood it. *"Are you not in error because you do not know the Scriptures or the power of God?... Have you not read in the Book of Moses?... You are badly mistaken!"* (Mark 12:24–27).

Jesus warned the Sadducees that their doubts were not caused by their living in a scientific age, but by their acting like a scientist who predicts the outcome of his experiments before he conducts them and rigs the results to support his prior assumptions. They had read the Scriptures so superficially that they had failed to grasp the true coherence of God's Word. They had passed judgment upon the very verses God intended to help them pass judgment upon themselves.

So don't make the mistake of acting like a Roman relativist, a Pharisee moralist or a Sadducee materialist. Read the Bible with the same humility as the disciples of Jesus. As you read their gospel accounts of Jesus' teaching, step out on the same faith-filled journey of discovery as they did. Respond to the same challenge Jesus laid down for them:

"If anyone chooses to do God's will" – in other words, if anybody decides to believe God's Word and to start putting it into practice every day – *"then they will find out whether or not my teaching comes from God"* (John 7:17). Remember, believing is seeing. Don't fall for other people's excuses. Jesus tells us that the best way to find out whether or not the Bible is full of myths and contradictions is to start living as if what it says is true.

CHAPTER 7
Hasn't Evolution Disproved God?

For many people, that last chapter doesn't give enough of an answer. Their big question is not about myths and contradictions in general. It is about one Bible passage in particular. How can anybody take the Christian faith seriously when the Bible starts by telling us that God created the world in just six days? This is such an important question that I've given it a separate chapter. Doesn't our modern understanding of evolution contradict the Bible's teaching about the Creator God?

It's worth noting that Jesus never talked about evolution. The idea only became popular after Charles Darwin published his book *On the Origin of Species* in 1859, reflecting on what he had seen of the world's flora and fauna during his five-year-long voyage on the HMS *Beagle* from England to Australia and back again:

> *In October 1838, that is, fifteen months after I had begun my systematic enquiry, I happened to read for amusement "Malthus on Population", and being*

well prepared to appreciate the struggle for existence which everywhere goes on from long-continued observation of the habits of animals and plants, it at once struck me that under these circumstances favourable variations would tend to be preserved, and unfavourable ones to be destroyed. The result of this would be the formation of new species. Here, then, I had at last got a theory by which to work.[1]

Jesus said nothing that outright contradicts this observation by Charles Darwin. In fact, Jesus encouraged his followers to believe that the study of science could teach them a great deal about God. *"Consider the ravens... Consider how the wild flowers grow"* (Luke 12:24, 27). *"Are not two sparrows sold for a penny? Yet not one of them will fall to the ground outside your Father's care.... So don't be afraid; you are worth more than many sparrows"* (Matthew 10:29, 31). Jesus even likened himself to King Solomon, the pioneering botanist and zoologist who had developed one of the world's first ever systems of classification for mammals, birds, reptiles and fish (1 Kings 4:33). Jesus told the crowds that they should listen to his teaching because *"one greater than Solomon is here"* (Luke 11:31).

But Jesus always expected scientific discovery to provoke bigger spiritual questions. He criticized the short-sighted Pharisees and Sadducees for looking at nature but never beyond it: *"When evening comes, you say, 'It will be fair weather, for the sky is red,' and in the*

1   He recalls this in *The Autobiography of Charles Darwin* (1887).

morning, 'Today it will be stormy, for the sky is red and overcast.' You know how to interpret the appearance of the sky, but you cannot interpret the signs of the times" (Matthew 16:2–3). They did not know, as we do, that the earth revolves around a sun a million times bigger than it is, that the sun is merely one of a hundred billion stars in the Milky Way, or that the Milky Way itself is merely one of over a hundred billion galaxies. Nevertheless, he expected even their limited grasp of science to whet their appetite to know what kind of being might have created all the wonders they saw. He expected them to be excited when he told them that *"at the beginning the Creator made them"* (Matthew 19:4). He expected them to listen to what he had to say about *"the beginning, when God created the world"* (Mark 13:19).

Jesus therefore warns us not to treat evolution as the final answer. How can it be? If all life on earth derived from a single simple life form, we ought to ask how that original creature came into being with such latently diverse DNA and how the solar system that supported it appeared in such perfection. If they emerged from a Big Bang that created all matter, we ought to ask what immaterial force initiated it: Who was the "Big Banger"? The more we discover of science, the more we ought to exclaim with Sir Isaac Newton in his groundbreaking scientific manual, *"This most beautiful System of the Sun, Planets and Comets, could only proceed from the counsel and dominion of an intelligent and powerful being."*[2]

2   Sir Isaac Newton wrote this in Book III of his *Principia* (1687).

There are plenty of evolutionists who see no contradiction between their science books and the Bible. The leading geneticist Francis Collins states his view simply: *"The God of the Bible is also the God of the genome. He can be worshipped in the cathedral or in the laboratory. His creation is majestic, awesome, intricate, and beautiful."*[3] The issue at stake here is therefore not whether belief in evolution rules out belief in the Creator God, but whether belief in evolution answers all of our questions by itself or whether it simply stirs our hunger to discover more about the vast uncharted territory that lies beyond evolution.

Shortly before he died, I had the privilege of spending an afternoon with the great British philosopher Antony Flew. I was keen to ask the famous atheist and author of *Darwinian Evolution* why, in his final years, he had become an unlikely advocate for the existence of God. He gave me the same explanation he gave in his final book:

> *I believe that this universe's intricate laws manifest what scientists have called the Mind of God. I believe that life and reproduction originate in a divine Source. Why do I believe this, given that I expounded and defended atheism for more than a half century? The short answer is this: this is the world picture, as I see it, that has emerged from modern science. Science spotlights three dimensions of nature that point to God. The first is the fact that nature obeys laws.*

3   Francis Collins in *The Language of God: A Scientist Presents Evidence for Belief* (2007).

The second is the dimension of life, of intelligently organized and purpose-driven beings, which arose from matter. The third is the very existence of nature.... When I finally came to recognize the existence of a God, it was not a paradigm shift, because my paradigm remains... "We must follow the argument wherever it leads."[4]

Antony Flew's desire to question the boundaries of science-as-religion made him enemies. When I met him, he had been rejected by most of his former colleagues and dismissed by the British newspapers as an old man going senile. But what science and Christianity have in common is that they always require courage. It isn't only popes who oppose new ideas. It is also professors, such as the Harvard geneticist Richard Lewontin, who confesses that *"We take the side of science **in spite** of the patent absurdity of some of its constructs... because we have a prior commitment, a commitment to materialism. It is not that the methods and institutions of science somehow compel us to accept a material explanation of the phenomenal world, but, on the contrary, that we are forced by our a priori adherence to material causes to create an apparatus of investigation and a set of concepts that produce material explanations, no matter how counter-intuitive, no matter how mystifying to the uninitiated. Moreover, that materialism is an absolute, for we cannot*

4   Antony Flew in *There Is a God: How the World's Most Notorious Atheist Changed His Mind* (2007).

allow a Divine Foot in the door."[5] The same Jesus who challenged his first-century listeners to force their way past reactionary rabbis and Caesar's censors also calls us to force our way past the self-appointed gamekeepers who tell us what questions we are and are not permitted to ask when we study science.

Francis Crick was forced to do this when he discovered the double helix of DNA. His discovery contradicted some major aspects of Charles Darwin's simple theory. Life was far more complex than Darwin could possibly have comprehended in his own day.[6] The difference between a fish and a bird and between a monkey and a human was infinitely greater than was imagined by the Victorians. Each tiny double helix is several trillion times smaller than the smallest piece of functional machinery ever built by humans, yet it contains all of the data required to specify the arrangement of over 200 bones, over 600 muscles, over 50,000 auditory nerve fibres, over 2 million optic nerve fibres, over a hundred thousand hairs, and over 35 trillion cells in each human body. After his discovery, Francis Crick warned the scientific community to develop some more humility: *"I would make this prophecy: what everyone believed yesterday, and you believe today, only cranks will believe tomorrow."*[7]

5   Richard Lewontin, writing in *The New York Review of Books* on 9th January 1997.

6   Do you see what I did there when I referred to the 19th century as "Darwin's day"? Christians take differing views over whether the "days" in Genesis 1 refer to 24-hour periods or to an unspecified period of time.

7   Francis Crick gave this prophecy in his book *Of Molecules and Men* (1966).

Jesus knew what he was doing when he commanded his listeners to believe that in the beginning, *"God created the world"* (Mark 13:19). He knew that every scientific breakthrough would become a fresh crossroads for the human race. Would we become intoxicated with our new discoveries, duped into thinking that our fractionally greater insight now means we have no further need for our Creator? Or would we find in our increasing scientific knowledge an increasing thirst for spiritual answers? Would it make us long to know the God who made the animals and birds and flowers and rocks and DNA? Jesus calls us to reject the smug self-satisfaction of modern science and to explore the many questions those who love science the most should naturally ask. He wants us to gain the same insight that provoked the author C. S. Lewis to conclude: *"In science we have been reading only the notes to a poem; in Christianity we find the poem itself."*[8]

Life is not a cosmic accident, devoid of meaning. It is derived from the God who made the universe in all its majesty. That's why Jesus told his followers excitedly to *"Go into all the world and preach the good news to all creation"* (Mark 16:15). Your Creator loves you and has sent his Son to earth in order to enable you to discover him and to enjoy knowing him forever.

8   C. S. Lewis in his book *Miracles* (1947).

CHAPTER 8

Why Doesn't God End Racism?

I love the way that growing up in one of the world's most multiracial cities has affected my children. A minority of the children in my son's class have English as their first language, so when he told me about his first day at school I instinctively asked him to describe the cultural backgrounds of his friends. It seemed like a perfectly normal adult question when I asked him, *"Is Shawn white or black?"* but he answered like a five-year-old. *"I really don't know, Dad, but I do know that he supports Tottenham Hotspur."*

Sadly, racial harmony is not as widespread across London as it is in my son's class at school. When white policemen shot and killed a black man in August 2011, it provoked an angry wave of rioting and looting across the city. When the predominantly white police force sent a black officer to intercede with the rioters, he was met with cries of *"Uncle Tom!"* and *"Coconut!"* Perhaps these racial tensions shouldn't surprise us, given that the British conquered much of the world in their pursuit of empire, or that 3,000 ships left London between 1698 and 1809 to transport 740,000 African slaves to America and the Caribbean. But what should surprise us is that in the era of those slave ships and conquering armies, the British churches were full every Sunday. If God created the human race as one big family, why does he permit such racism to continue?

How big a question this is for you probably depends on how much you have been on the receiving end of racism. If you are white and live in the same country as your great-grandparents, it may not seem like a question worth asking Jesus at all. However, if you are not white or if you live in a different country from the one in which you were born then it is likely to be a huge question. It is certainly one that Jesus is very happy to answer. He lived in a violently racist culture and he was a vocal opponent of racism in its many different forms.

The Romans made the British look like amateurs at imperialism. They even had an insulting term for the non-Romans that they conquered. They were barbarians. They singled out the Jewish nation for particular hatred, exiling the Jews from Rome altogether in 19 AD and 49 AD. The Jews returned the favour. Their leaders did not hesitate to crucify the Messiah but they baulked at the thought of entering Governor Pontius Pilate's palace in order to do so (John 18:28). Peter told a gathering of Romans that *"It is against our law for a Jew to associate with or visit a Gentile. But God has shown me that I should not call anyone impure or unclean"* (Acts 10:27–2; see also 11:2–3). The whole point of Jesus' famous parable about the Good Samaritan is that Jews and Samaritans hated one another. They were about as likely to help one another as a Black Panther and a Ku Klux Klansman. Jesus launched a full-frontal attack on this openly and unashamedly racist culture.

One of the most famous commands of Jesus in the gospels is to *"Love your neighbour as yourself"*.[1] Most people are aware that Jesus gave this command but they are largely unaware that it is why he told the Parable of the Good Samaritan. Jesus used it to label interracial tension as the bitter fruit of human sin. Adam's first sin was quickly followed by one of his sons murdering the other. His family was divided into factions at the Tower of Babel and those factions soon started waging war against one another. Jesus told his followers that he had come into the world to destroy the self-destructive power of human sin. He promised to reconcile people back to God and, in doing so, to reconcile them to each other too. *"Whoever claims to love God yet hates a brother or sister is a liar. For whoever does not love their brother and sister, whom they have seen, cannot love God, whom they have not seen"* (1 John 4:20). The hero in the Parable of the Good Samaritan is the one who sees past ethnic prejudice to embrace a hated foreigner as a beloved brother.

1   This was actually a quotation from Leviticus 19:18. Jesus quotes it in Matthew 5:43, 19:19 and 22:39, and in Mark 12:31. He provokes other people to quote it in Mark 12:33 and Luke 10:27.

I have seen this miracle in action, not just in the innocence of my five-year-old son but also in the hearts of many of the adults at the church I lead in London. I have seen elderly Afrikaners, once strong supporters of apartheid, embracing the black Africans in the church as their brothers and sisters. I had the privilege of praying with a Jamaican woman whose ancestors were kidnapped and transported across the Atlantic to work in the sugar plantations. At the end of a sermon I preached on racism, she quoted Genesis 50:20 and told me that she had finally forgiven the white slave traders for what they had done to her family: *"They intended to harm us, but God intended it for good."*

We therefore need to think before we criticize Jesus for not speaking out more strongly against slavery. We need to do our research. Most first-century slaves were prisoners of war who would have been slaughtered on the battlefield had they not been taken to the slave markets instead.[2] Unlike New World slavery, most Roman slaves could win back their freedom within a decade. Their standard of living was often higher as slaves than it had been before, since their masters had a vested interest in providing for their needs. The Communist pioneer Friedrich Engels was right to point out that sudden liberation would have made their lot in life much harder: *"The slave is sold once and for all; the proletarian must sell*

2   The Roman jurist Gaius tells us this straightforwardly in his *Institutes* (161 AD).

63

himself daily and hourly. The individual slave, property of one master, is assured an existence, however miserable it may be, because of the master's interest. The individual proletarian, property as it were of the entire bourgeois class which buys his labour only when someone has need of it, has no secure existence…. Thus, the slave can have a better existence than the proletarian."[3]

Instead of attacking slavery as an institution, Jesus did something far more radical. He undermined it through the way he lived and died. Although he was the Son of God, he accepted the lowest place in society. The apostle Paul tells us literally that *"Being in very nature God, he did not consider equality with God something to be grasped. Rather, he made himself nothing by taking the very nature of a slave"* (Philippians 2:6–7). Jesus told the Jews to humble themselves with him, for they would only be forgiven their sins if they had as much faith as the hated Romans (Matthew 8:10–12). He told the Samaritans to humble themselves too, for they would only be saved if they listened to the hated Jews (John 4:22). Jesus paved the humble road towards true freedom when he died on a cross – the death normally reserved for runaway slaves and for the lowest of the low.

Jesus gave such radical teaching about human brotherhood that his followers have been the biggest

3   Friedrich Engels wrote this in *The Principles of Communism* (1847), which was adapted by Karl Marx the following year into *The Communist Manifesto* (1848).

opponents of slavery for the past 2,000 years.[4] However, he did far more than protest against a corrupt system. He laid down his life in order to destroy the deep-seated racism that lay at its core. His disciple John records what happened three days before his crucifixion.

> Now there were some Greeks among those who went up to worship at the festival. They came to Philip, who was from Bethsaida in Galilee, with a request. "Sir," they said, "we would like to see Jesus." Philip went to tell Andrew; Andrew and Philip in turn told Jesus. Jesus replied, "The hour has come for the Son of Man to be glorified…. Now is the time for judgment on this world; now the prince of this world will be driven out. And I, when I am lifted up from the earth, will draw all people to "myself". (John 12:20–33)

Note what happens here. Some Greeks arrive at the Jewish Temple and find themselves barred from celebrating the Passover. They turn to Philip, a Jewish disciple of Jesus who has a Greek name and is therefore likely to sympathize with them. Philip enlists the help of Andrew, another Jewish disciple with a Greek name, and they both tell Jesus that Greeks want to become part of God's Family too. Jesus gets excited. He declares that the moment the whole world has been waiting for has finally arrived. He is about to destroy the Devil's princely power

4   Paul taught that slaves were equal to their masters (Galatians 3:28 and Ephesians 6:9). He outlawed the slave trade and encouraged many masters to free their slaves (1 Timothy 1:10 and Philemon 16). That's why Christian Europe quickly outlawed slavery, and when the curse returned during the colonization of the New World, it's why Christian politicians led the fight for its abolition.

over humanity and draw people from every nation into God's glorious multiracial family. But there is a price tag. Before this can happen, Jesus must be lifted up on a cross. He must break the power that sin has wielded in the hearts of humans since Adam sinned in the Garden of Eden. He must confront sin's power by paying sin's penalty in order to drive sin's curse out of this world for good.

The apostle Paul explains what happened when Jesus died. *"Sin entered the world through one man, and death through sin, and in this way death came to all people, because all sinned... So also one righteous act resulted in justification and life for all people. For just as through the disobedience of the one man the many were made sinners, so also through the obedience of the one man the many will be made righteous"* (Romans 5:12–19). Paul tells us that the entire human race has been levelled through the fact that Jesus needed to die on the cross for our sin. It doesn't matter if we are black or white, Jewish or Gentile, British or Bolivian. The cross calls us all to get down on our knees and to confess that we have sinned against God. It's hard to look down on someone else when you are on your knees before God. Having been adopted by grace into God's Family, it is hard to feel superior about secondary issues such as nationality, gender or freedom. People who truly know that God has reconciled them to himself are always willing to be reconciled to one another.

Make no mistake. To be racist is to support the Devil's bid to reign as prince of this world. To love people from every nation is to be like Jesus. That's why those who have come to know Jesus across the past 2,000 years have always been the greatest opponents of racism. Look at the apostle Paul, at William Wilberforce, at Abraham Lincoln and at Martin Luther King. Then add your own name alongside theirs.

CHAPTER 9

Isn't God Prudish and Homophobic?

Watching the Benedict Cumberbatch and Keira Knightley movie *The Imitation Game* can tell you a lot about yourself. How do you respond to the story of Alan Turing, the brilliant British mathematician who helped defeat the Nazis during World War Two by cracking their Enigma code and who was later bullied into suicide because he was gay?

Many people respond with indignation. How could the British treat one of their war heroes so shabbily? Other people respond with a very different sort of indignation. How dare Hollywood attempt to rewrite the history of World War Two, overegging the pain of Alan Turing's breakup with Joan Clarke in order to turn him into a gay martyr? Whichever type of indignation you feel, it's important that you understand that Jesus sides with neither of these two extremes. Jesus has placed himself precisely where we want him to answer our biggest questions, so let's also place ourselves where he wants us too. Let's listen to what he has to say.

For a start, let's admit frankly that Jesus never said anything in support of gay rights. He never even mentioned homosexuality, which is rather odd given that he spoke out so clearly against racism, traditionalism and religious hypocrisy. Although a few fringe scholars claim that he chose twelve male disciples because he was attracted to men, there is a reason why nobody else has claimed this during the past 2,000 years of history. His enemies sought to discredit him in every conceivable way but even they never attempted to lodge this type of allegation against him. Everybody knew that he was not a gay-rights activist.

But at the same time, let's admit frankly that Jesus does not condone the homophobic hate preachers. There was a group of people who hated the gay and the sexually promiscuous. They were called the Pharisees and Jesus reserved his fiercest rebukes for them. Let's look at one of Jesus' fieriest encounters with them, in John 8:2–11.

> At dawn Jesus appeared again in the temple courts, where all the people gathered round him, and he sat down to teach them. The teachers of the law and the Pharisees brought in a woman caught in adultery. They made her stand before the group and said to Jesus, "Teacher, this woman was caught in the act of adultery. In the Law Moses commanded us to stone such women. Now what do you say?" They were using this question as a trap, in order to have a basis for accusing him.
>
> But Jesus bent down and started to write on the ground with his finger. When they kept on questioning him, he straightened up and said to them, "Let any one of you who

*is without sin be the first to throw a stone at her." Again
he stooped down and wrote on the ground.*

*At this, those who heard began to go away one at a
time, the older ones first, until only Jesus was left, with
the woman still standing there. Jesus straightened up
and asked her, "Woman, where are they? Has no one
condemned you?"*

"No one, sir," she said.

*"Then neither do I condemn you," Jesus declared. "Go
now and leave your life of sin."*

We live in a culture that is both aggressively pro-
gay and aggressively homophobic, both sexually
promiscuous and sexually judgmental. We live in a
culture that wants Jesus to take sides, so it is vital that
we take clashes like this one seriously. What does Jesus
teach us about God? Is he prudish and homophobic or
is he as easy-going as Western culture? Let's make a
few simple observations.

First, Jesus *refuses to label the woman*. The Pharisees
loved to label people so that they could write them
off as people who didn't matter deeply to God. That
one is an adulterer. She's a prostitute. He is gay. She's
a lesbian. He's a leper. He's a no-good tax collector.
The Devil loves it when we label people in a way that
assumes that their past and present allows them no
hope of change in the future. But Jesus did not label
this woman as an "adulteress" any more than he
labelled the five-times-married woman at the well as a
"slut" or Pontius Pilate as a "foreigner". That kind of
label always imprisons and never saves. In the same

way, Jesus refuses to label people as gay or lesbian or bisexual or straight. He reaches deep beneath the label to offer every individual a future brimful of hope. He looks at the person standing before him and simply addresses her as *"Woman"*.

Second, Jesus *refuses to compromise God's holy character*. These verses tell us that the Pharisees asked this question in order to trap Jesus. They hoped to trick him into contradicting the Old Testament's clear teaching about sex – that God created men and women differently and called them to reflect God's love for humanity by treating sex as God's great wedding present, reserved for marriage between one man and one woman for the whole of their lives. No sexually transmitted diseases. No unwanted pregnancies or traumatic abortions. No sexual baggage carried into marriage and no sexual betrayal once inside. Jesus does not fall for their trap. Not only does he fully affirm the Old Testament's teaching about sex, he confronts the woman with her sexual sin.[1] This isn't the first time that she has sinned and fallen under God's judgment. Jesus warns her, *"Go now and leave your life of sin."*

But note thirdly that Jesus *refuses to place sexual sin in a separate category to other sins*. He tells her to leave her life of sin – not just her adulterous relationship, but also her entire self-centred lifestyle that is so

1   Matthew 19:4–6 echoes Leviticus 18:22 and 20:13, and is in turn echoed by Romans 1:26–27 and 1 Timothy 1:9–10. Jesus affirms this further in Matthew 19:10–12 by encouraging people who do not wish to be married for life to a person of the opposite sex to embrace singleness as a worthy, honourable God-given calling.

displeasing to God. In order to emphasize that every sin is serious, Jesus bends down and starts writing in the dust. Although the passage does not tell us what he wrote, many Bible scholars believe that he wrote the Ten Commandments: make pleasing God your number-one priority, stop trying to twist God's character to conform to your own preferences, stop using swear words, stop being so crazy-busy, and respect the wisdom of your parents. That's just the first five. Jesus stands up and looks the Pharisees in the eye. Do you still want to stone her to death for her sin? *"Let any one of you who is without sin be the first to throw a stone at her."*

Jesus bends down and gives them the other five. Don't murder – they have stones in their hands. Don't commit adultery – each one of them has fantasized about having sex with somebody other than his wife. Do not steal. Do not lie. Do not burn with jealousy to possess something that belongs to someone else. Jesus stands up again and finds that every single stone-wielding Pharisee has slunk away. Only the woman is left.

Jesus refuses to indulge our culture's rejection of every sexual boundary. How could he, when the terrible results of our sexual experiments are everywhere – in broken homes, in unwanted babies, in unloved wives and in abused children? But don't let his confrontation of our sin make you think he sides with the stone-wielding Pharisees. He bitterly opposes them. He will oppose us too if we condemn the *"gay"* in gay pride without confessing that *"pride"* lurks in all our hearts. None of us is straight. Every single one of us is sexually crooked. You may not drool over pictures on the internet, you may not masturbate in secret, you may not indulge in sexual daydreams, you may not flirt and you may not follow through on your same-sex attraction – but you are not completely sinless sexually. When we point the finger at other people's sin, we are as ridiculous as the Pharisees when they tried to stone a woman caught in the act of adultery while allowing the man caught with her to get away with it scot-free.

Fourth, note that Jesus *responds lovingly to the woman's humble repentance*. He meets humility with love and forgiveness, never with anger. He commands the woman to leave her life of sin because he truly believes he can empower her to change. He can transform her life so completely through the Holy Spirit that she will become like all the others that the Devil tried to label but that Jesus dared to save. The prostitute we now know as Mary Magdalene. The tax collector we now know as the gospel writer Matthew. The murderer we now know as the apostle Paul. Our churches must not jar God's ears with words of homophobia and moral finger-pointing. They must echo the words of Jesus to this woman: *"Neither do I condemn you. Go now and leave your life of sin."*

It was these faith-filled words that brought hope to a first-century world that had learned to accept promiscuity and adultery and homosexuality as simply part and parcel of the human condition. It was these words that created churches that brought real hope to a world that was waking up to the hangover of its own sexual revolution. The apostle Paul was able to tell the followers of Jesus, *"Do not be deceived: neither the sexually immoral nor idolaters nor adulterers nor men who have sex with men nor thieves nor the greedy nor drunkards nor slanderers nor swindlers will inherit the kingdom of God. And that is what some of you were. But you were washed, you were sanctified, you were justified in the name of the Lord Jesus Christ and by the Spirit of our God"* (1 Corinthians 6:9–11).

Jesus may empower you to fall in love with somebody of the opposite sex, just as he did my friend Mark when he decided to resist same-sex attraction in order to follow Jesus. Jesus may empower you to rekindle love in your loveless marriage, just as he did my friend Carol when she fell out of love with her husband. Alternatively he may empower you to walk the same path as my friend Jamie, finding satisfaction in God even as he continues to fight same-sex attraction, or my friend Robert as he finds satisfaction in God in the midst of a loveless marriage.[2]

Jesus isn't out to spoil your fun. He wants to give you something better than the fleeting joys of sex and the inconstant idol of a happy marriage. He refuses to allow your sex life to define who you are. *"I do not condemn you. Go now and leave your life of sin."*

2   Two books for further reading that Jamie would recommend if you are walking the same path as him are *Is God Anti-Gay?* by Sam Allberry (2013) and *The Plausibility Problem* by Ed Shaw (2015).

CHAPTER 10
Isn't the God of the Old Testament Immoral?

My family owns what surely has to be the weirdest ever children's Bible. I don't know who decided which stories to include and which stories to leave out, but what I do know is that they made some seriously odd choices. One evening, I read two pages side by side. The left-hand page recounted the Ten Commandments, which God gave to Moses on Mount Sinai: do not steal, do not lie, do not commit adultery, do not kill. The right-hand page described how God commanded Moses to attack the Midianites: *"The Lord said to Moses, 'Take vengeance on the Midianites'... They fought against Midian, as the Lord commanded Moses, and killed every man."* I often fool around at bedtime, so my children immediately started laughing. They told me to stop joking and to read the Bible properly. But I was reading the Bible properly. That's the problem.

Old Testament passages such as the massacre of the Midianites in Numbers 31 give plenty of ammunition to those who want to reject the Bible. Richard Dawkins makes much of them in his book *The God Delusion*. He argues that *"The God of the Old Testament is arguably the most unpleasant character in all fiction:... a vindictive, bloodthirsty ethnic cleanser; a misogynistic, homophobic, racist, infanticidal, genocidal, filicidal, pestilential, megalomaniacal, sadomasochistic, capriciously malevolent bully."* So, is he right?

Most of us expect Jesus to try to duck out of answering this question. Despite his frank responses so far, we imagine that this time he will look embarrassed, clear his throat, and mumble, *"I was afraid that you were going to ask me that."* But Jesus does not duck this question any more than he did the others. He looks us straight in the eye and tells us: *"Do not think that I have come to abolish the Law or the Prophets; I have not come to abolish them but to fulfil them. For truly I tell you, until heaven and earth disappear, not the smallest letter, not the least stroke of a pen, will by any means disappear from the Law until everything is accomplished. Therefore anyone who sets aside one of the least of these commands and teaches others accordingly will be called least in the kingdom of heaven"* (Matthew 5:17–19).

Now that's remarkable. Whenever people dismiss the God of the Old Testament as an immoral monster, they tend to point to Jesus' longest and most famous sermon, the Sermon on the Mount. However little you know about the teaching of Jesus, you will know quotations from what is widely regarded as the greatest piece of moral teaching in human history: *"Turn the other cheek... Go the extra mile... Love your enemies... Do to others what you would have them do to you"* (Matthew 5–7). Yet note that Jesus gives this complete affirmation of the Old Testament at the beginning of the Sermon on the Mount. He sees his moral teaching not as correction, but as further explanation.

Jesus is able to answer our question because he studied the Old Testament so deeply that, even as a twelve-year-old, he flabbergasted the greatest rabbis (Luke 2:47). He tells us that our problems stem from the fact that we have read the Old Testament far too superficially. We are offended that God commands Moses to slaughter the Midianites, failing to notice that Moses was himself a genocide survivor! However hard I find it to read these verses to my children as we sit on a comfortable bed in London, it was far harder for Moses to write them when he thought back to how close he had come to dying in Pharaoh's slaughter of the Hebrew babies. If this were not bad enough, Moses was also married to a Midianite woman and had lived for forty years with her family in Midian. His nephews and nieces were Midianites. His own sons were half-Midianite. He probably spoke fluent Midianite and had preached about the Lord to the Midianites on many occasions. Are you offended by what God told Moses to do? Then Moses tells you to spare him the shocked face. Get to the back of the queue. He was far more offended than you are.

We discover why Moses followed through on God's command when we read the Old Testament a little more carefully. In Genesis 19 and Leviticus 18,

Moses describes what it was like to live among the Canaanites and Midianites. They were gang rapists. They murdered their babies in sordid sacrifices to their gods. They were drunkards and idolaters and slave traders and child abusers and incestuous sexual perverts. God never commanded genocide. Achan the Hebrew died for covering up his sin, whereas Rahab the Canaanite prostitute was spared for confessing hers (Joshua 6–7). The conquest of Canaan was never about ethnic cleansing; it was always about spiritual purity. It was never about race; it was always about repentance. God's judgment fell on communities of sinners in the Old Testament as a picture of a greater Judgment Day that is coming.

That's why Jesus never distances himself from any of these Old Testament stories. He affirms them both as events in the past and as sobering warnings for the present. He takes two of the most offensive examples – Noah's Flood and the destruction of Sodom – and he warns us: *"Just as it was in the days of Noah, so also will it be in the days of the Son of Man. People were eating, drinking, marrying and being given in marriage up to the day Noah entered the ark. Then the flood came and destroyed them all. It was the same in the days of Lot. People were eating and drinking, buying and selling, planting and building. But the day Lot left Sodom, fire and sulphur rained down from heaven and destroyed them all. It will be just like this on the day the Son of Man is revealed"* (Luke 17:26–30). Jesus is the Son of Man and he is coming back to judge the world. These events warn us that God will not turn a blind eye to unconfessed sin forever.

Far from backpedalling in the Sermon on the Mount, Jesus reveals additional shocking detail about the Judgment Day that is coming. He speaks so lovingly of God's forgiveness that even the atheist novelist Kurt Vonnegut exclaimed that *"If Christ hadn't delivered the Sermon on the Mount, with its message of mercy and pity, I wouldn't want to be a human being"*, but his offer of forgiveness comes with urgency.[1] God makes the offer because we need it. Jesus warns us that if we reject this message of salvation then we will have nothing left to save us from the fierceness of God's justice when it comes. He says in Matthew 5:21–30:

> *"You have heard that it was said to the people [in the Old Testament], 'You shall not murder, and anyone who murders will be subject to judgment.' But I tell you that anyone who is angry with a brother or sister… will be in danger of the fire of hell…. You have heard that it was said, 'You shall not commit adultery.' But I tell you that anyone who looks at a woman lustfully has already committed adultery with her in his heart. If your right eye causes you to stumble, gouge it out and throw it away. It is better for you to lose one part of your body than for your whole body to be thrown into hell. And if your right hand causes you to stumble, cut it off and throw it away. It is better for you to lose one part of your body than for your whole body to go into hell."*

---

1   Kurt Vonnegut in his book of essays *A Man Without a Country* (2005).

Read those verses slowly. They are terrifying. But Jesus doesn't rush to apologize. He wants us to grasp the bad news because, without it, we will fail to grasp the good news. God will not permit us to behave as though we were little gods, demanding that the world revolve around us. He has set a day when he will judge every person who tries to usurp the place that belongs to him and him alone. He delays that Judgment Day because he wants to give us time to repent of our sin – that is, to confess that we have done wrong, that we need to be forgiven and that we need to commit our lives to serving him from this moment on. If you have already repented and become part of God's Family, he wants to give you time to issue this same urgent command to your friends and family and neighbours: *Get ready. God's Judgment Day is coming.*

Unless we understand the utter darkness of our position before God, we will never appreciate the true value of the dawning of God's mercy. Kurt Vonnegut admired the beauty of Jesus' teaching about God's mercy and pity, but he never responded to them because he chose to ignore Jesus' teaching about God's justice. Like many of the sinful people groups in the Old Testament who were given time to repent before their Day of Judgment (for example, in Genesis 15:16), Vonnegut mistook delay for double-mindedness and confused God's patience with his being a pushover. He ignored the message of the Old Testament that God will not tolerate our sins forever.

Now for the good news. Jesus told his followers that he had come from heaven to earth in order to become the Saviour that we desperately need. When he died on the cross, he created an alternative place where God's judgment can fall on sinners. We can bear the penalty for our wrongdoing ourselves, or we can trust that Jesus bore the penalty for us when he died a criminal's death. Jesus has put himself right where we want him – quite literally. He has died in our place and experienced our Judgment Day so that we don't have to. Whenever we eat bread and drink wine as an expression of our faith in his nail-pierced body and his blood-stained cross, we say yes to his Gospel invitation: *"Drink from it, all of you. This is my blood of the covenant, which is poured out for many for the forgiveness of sins"* (Matthew 26:27–28).

Jesus has not shrunk from answering our question. Now he has a question of his own. How will we respond to his great act of mercy towards us? Will we complain that God was unfair to judge sinners in the Old Testament or will we treat those events as prophetic warnings that a far worse Judgment Day is coming? Will we shake our fist at God because he dares to judge our sin, or will we raise our hands in worship that he dared to come and bear the judgment in our place?

God is not immoral. We are. That's the message that got Jesus killed, but it's the message that brings us life.

CHAPTER 11
How Can a Loving God Judge People?

O n 4th October 2014, ISIS fighters attacked the Syrian town of Kobani with chemical weapons. Bazran Halil managed to escape over the border into Turkey to describe what he saw: *"People literally burned from the inside out… There was a man with Down Syndrome. He couldn't understand the situation, to flee, or to run away from the frontline. When ISIS arrived they beheaded him and took photos, shared them on social media and said, 'We killed an atheist, a Kaffir.'"*

One of his neighbours, Mostafa Kader, also managed to escape to tell his story. As he fled, he found the bodies of his wife's sister and his eight-year-old niece, lying together in pools of blood. *"They had been raped, and their hearts were cut out of their chests and left on top of the bodies. I buried them with my own hands…. It would be better to have died in Kobani."*

I don't want to upset you, but I do want to help you understand why Jesus doesn't answer all of our big questions in the manner we expect. He has answered our first ten questions at face value, but this one is different. It is the only question he corrects before he answers. Jesus does not rush to justify the Bible's teaching about the great Judgment Day that is coming. Instead, he asks us to get a bigger picture of the world. People at dinner parties in Western cities may complain that God has vowed to judge the world, but they don't complain at dinner parties in Kobani. The far bigger question which has been asked throughout human history is: In view of all the terrible wickedness in the world, how can a loving God *not* judge people?

That's one of the reasons why I love living in a city that is home to people from so many different nations. My friends who fled to London from the Congolese Civil War and from the genocide in Rwanda never ask me how a loving God can judge people. They only ever ask me how a loving God could have failed to prevent the atrocities they saw. The same is true of friends who escaped to London from Afghanistan and Iraq and North Korea, but you don't have to be a non-European to appreciate this bigger perspective. The Croatian thinker Miroslav Volf reflected after the civil war that devastated his Yugoslavian homeland in the 1990s that *"If God were not angry at injustice and deception and did not make the final end to violence, God would not be worthy of our worship.... My thesis that the practice of nonviolence requires a belief in divine vengeance will be unpopular with many... in the West.... [but] it takes the quiet of a suburban home for the birth of the thesis that human non-violence corresponds to God's refusal to judge.*

In a scorched land, soaked in the blood of the innocent, it will invariably die.... [along with] many other pleasant captivities of the liberal mind."[1]

This eleventh question is therefore different from the ten that have gone before. Jesus warns us not to allow our Western comforts to cloud our thinking into treating hell as an offensive doctrine – fine in medieval paintings and in episodes of *The Simpsons*, but not in God's plans to restore justice to the world. Jesus warns us not to wish short-sightedly that God were a corrupt judge who lacks the character to insist that justice must prevail. He urges us to listen to the anguished cries of those who suffer around the world. A God who did not punish Adolf Hitler for gassing 6 million Jews and ISIS fighters for raping eight-year-old girls would not be worthy of our worship. He would be a corrupt monster. The real God gets angry with sin and vows to punish it. That's good news. Rebecca Pippert reminds us: *"God's wrath is not a cranky explosion, but his settled opposition to the cancer of sin which is eating out the insides of the human race he loves with his whole being."*[2]

To help us understand the glory of God's justice, Jesus told three simple parables. The first one explains why God does not eliminate all of the evil in the world straightaway. It is the Parable of the Weeds in Matthew 13:24–30. A farmer sows high-quality wheat in his field in order to produce tasty bread and cake for many people, but his enemy creeps into the field and

1   Miroslav Volf in his book *Exclusion and Embrace* (1996).
2   Rebecca Manley Pippert in her book *Hope Has Its Reasons* (1990).

sows weeds among the wheat. The farmer's servants come and tell him that his harvest field has become contaminated. Should they go through the field and rip out all the weeds? The farmer says no. If they rip out the weeds then they will also uproot the wheat. Instead, they must wait until harvest time. On that appointed day, the farmer will separate the wheat from the weeds, bringing the good seed into his barns and throwing the weeds onto the fire.

Note that in this parable Jesus expects our big question not to be *How can a loving God judge people?* but rather *How can a loving God wait so long before judging people?* Jesus corrects our question because he wants to challenge us. If we are asking the wrong question, it is a sign that we are part of the problem. It is a sign that our hearts have become so contaminated by sin that we have learned to accept our sinful world. Instead of being horrified at human wrongdoing, we are horrified that God should have the audacity to intervene. The Parable of the Weeds tells us that this is why God has delayed his Judgment Day for so long. If he eradicated all of the evil from the world in an instant, you would not be here to read this book and I would certainly not be here to write it. Evil is not just something "out there" in news reports about crime and civil wars. It is something deep within our own hearts. We are all wrongdoers. God holds off his judgment because he loves us and wants to save us.

The second parable is in Luke 16:19–31. Jesus deals with the fact that most of us are happy for God to judge the likes of Adolf Hitler and ISIS, just so long as he doesn't threaten to judge respectable people like you and me. Jesus tells us that *"There was a rich man who was dressed in purple and fine linen and lived in luxury every day. At his gate was laid a beggar named Lazarus, covered with sores and longing to eat what fell from the rich man's table. Even the dogs came and licked his sores. The time came when the beggar died and the angels carried him to Abraham's side. The rich man also died and was buried. In hell, where he was in torment, he looked up and saw Abraham far away, with Lazarus by his side."*

We are meant to do a double take when we read this. In hell, where he was in torment? Why?! What harm did the rich man ever do to anyone? He hasn't raped anyone, murdered anyone, committed adultery or blasphemed God's name. He hasn't done anything. Actually, Jesus tells us that's the problem. Sin is more than doing wrong; it is also failing to do what is right. The rich man is self-centred and complacent. He is so absorbed with the comforts of his own life that he thinks little about God and even less about the beggar at his gate. The problem is not his wealth. Abraham was fabulously rich, yet he is pictured in heaven. The problem is that the rich man has failed to spot the dangers of comfortable living. That's the tragic irony when many Westerners complain that God should dare to judge them. In view of our generation's unparalleled potential to make a difference right across the world, how could a loving God *not* judge us?

This makes uncomfortable reading, so Jesus follows it up with a third parable in Matthew 25:31–46. Jesus prophesies about the day when he will return to earth from heaven:

"When the Son of Man comes in his glory, and all the angels with him, he will sit on his glorious throne. All the nations will be gathered before him, and he will separate the people one from another as a shepherd separates the sheep from the goats. He will put the sheep on his right and the goats on his left. Then the King will say to those on his right, 'Come, you who are blessed by my Father; take your inheritance, the kingdom prepared for you since the creation of the world. For I was hungry and you gave me something to eat, I was thirsty and you gave me something to drink, I was a stranger and you invited me in, I needed clothes and you clothed me, I was sick and you looked after me, I was in prison and you came to visit me.'

"Then the righteous will answer him, 'Lord, when did we see you hungry and feed you, or thirsty and give you something to drink? When did we see you a stranger and invite you in, or needing clothes and clothe you? When did we see you sick or in prison and go to visit you?' The King will reply, 'Truly I tell you, whatever you did for one of the least of these brothers and sisters of mine, you did for me.'

"Then he will say to those on his left, 'Depart from me, you who are cursed, into the eternal fire prepared for the devil and his angels. For I was hungry and you gave me nothing to eat, I was thirsty and you gave me nothing to drink, I was a stranger and you did not invite me in, I needed clothes and you did not clothe me, I was sick and in prison and you did not look after me.' They also will

answer, 'Lord, when did we see you hungry or thirsty or
a stranger or needing clothes or sick or in prison, and did
not help you?' He will reply, 'Truly I tell you, whatever
you did not do for one of the least of these, you did not do
for me.' Then they will go away to eternal punishment,
but the righteous to eternal life."

The Parable of the Sheep and the Goats tells us that
God did not create hell for you and me. He created it
as a place of punishment for the Devil and his demons.
The only people who will ever go to hell are those
who side with the Devil, either through their active
wickedness or through their fatal complacency. Jesus
warns us that he will not judge us based on our good
intentions or on our own spiritual self-assessment. He
will judge us based on what we did and didn't do.
Divine justice will prevail.

But at least we got one thing right in our question.
Our Judge is indeed a loving God. Long before we
ever asked the question, the Lord found the perfect
answer to it. How can a loving God not judge goats
like you and me? By becoming a perfect, sinless sheep
– the one that John the Baptist called *"the Lamb of God,*
who takes away the sin of the world" (John 1:29) – and
by dying in the place of judgment for us. Jesus was
slaughtered like a goat so that we could be counted
among God's sheep.

How can a loving God not judge people? Only
through the death of his own Son. Jesus expects us to
receive this as the good news that it is:

For God so loved the world that he gave his one and only Son, that whoever believes in him shall not perish but have eternal life. (John 3:16)

In the end, the only people that God judges will be those who turn up their noses at his gift of life and, in rejecting his mercy, insist on receiving his justice instead.

CHAPTER 12
How Can There Only Be One True Way to God?

If I get in my car and drive a mile south from my house, I arrive at the largest mosque in Europe. If I turn north-east and drive for another three miles, I reach the second largest mosque in Europe. But here's the strange thing: both groups of Muslims believe that the other group are infidels who are going to hell. To people on the outside, that seems arrogant and blinkered and more than a little odd.

Back in my car, within a mile I have reached a Hindu temple. Just beyond it are a Jewish synagogue, an enormous Buddhist temple and the global headquarters of a splinter sect of Islam. All along my journey, I turn left and right at churches of every denomination. It's therefore hardly surprising that if the people in my city give religion any thought at all, they assume that there must be many different ways in which a person can find God. They agree with Oprah Winfrey when she observed on her talk show that *"One of the biggest mistakes humans make is to believe that there is only one way.… There are many… paths leading to what you call God."*[1] So, does Jesus agree?

If you have been following Jesus' responses so far, you know that his answer is a resounding no. If there were any other way to God without his having to die, Jesus would have directed his followers to choose that option from the religious menu instead. The closest option would have been Judaism, yet Jesus was very clear that Jews need his cross as much as anybody else. This raises a big question for us. Is Jesus as blinkered in his thinking as the rival Muslim factions in my city? How can anybody in our multifaith society truly believe that there is only one true way to God?

When we ask this question, we assume that our own culture is unique. We forget that Jesus was raised in a part of the world known as "Galilee of the Gentiles". It was home to Jews and Samaritans and Syro-Phoenicians and Greeks and Romans, who worshipped hundreds of different gods and goddesses between them. Jesus taught in a context of immense religious diversity and he affirmed what is obvious as I drive around my city. He took it as read that there are many different gods and many different pathways to them. He reinforced this with a quotation from Psalm 82. *"Jesus answered them, 'Is it not written in your Law, "I have said you are 'gods'?"'"* (John 10:34). Instead of challenging the fact that there are many different pathways, Jesus took a step back and asked people to sense-check whether they were truly worshipping the real God.

1   Oprah Winfrey said this on her talk show in 1998.

The Syro-Phoenicians worshipped the Canaanite god Baal-Zebub, so Jesus warned them that *"I do not drive out demons by Baal-Zebub… I drive out demons by the Spirit of God"* (Matthew 12:27–28). Jesus did not doubt their sincerity. They loved Baal-Zebub. He simply warned them that his miracles proved that they were trying to reach a false god and that the real God was trying to catch their attention.

The Greeks and Romans worshipped the pagan gods of Mount Olympus. Again, Jesus did not question their religious sincerity. They built magnificent temples and they prayed such long and devout prayers that Jesus had to warn the crowds, *"When you pray, do not keep on babbling like pagans, for they think they will be heard because of their many words"* (Matthew 6:7). Magnificent roads are of no use to a traveller unless they lead to where he wants to go. Jesus warned the pagans that their magnificent prayers were useless because they were not directed towards the real God.

The Jews claimed to worship the God of the Old Testament, but Jesus pointed out that they had modified his character to suit their own desires. He warned the Temple rulers, *"You are in error because you do not know the Scriptures or the power of God"* (Matthew 22:29). He warned the synagogue rulers, *"You shut the door of the kingdom of heaven in people's faces. You yourselves do not enter, nor will you let those enter who are trying to"* (Matthew 23:13). We need to take this to heart whenever people react with horror to the suggestion that all religions may not be equally valid.

Jesus was not crucified for telling pithy parables or for his witty social commentary. He was crucified because he challenged people that they were worshipping false gods.

This made Jesus powerful enemies. Who did this Galilean carpenter think he was to claim that there is only one real God and that he alone reveals God's character to the world? Jesus did not backpedal when he saw that they were offended. He performed miracles that proved he was far more than a Galilean carpenter and that they needed to take him seriously. He fed 5,000 people with five loaves of bread and two fish. He touched corpses and brought people back to life. He brought instant healing to those who were infected with incurable diseases such as leprosy. He explained to the crowds that these were all signs that he was far more than a prophet or guru or religious teacher. These signs proved he was the Son of God who had come into the world. *"I and the Father are one"* (John 10:30). *"Anyone who has seen me has seen the Father.... The words I say to you are not just my own. Rather, it is the Father, living in me, who is doing his work. Believe me when I say that I am in the Father and the Father is in me; or at least believe on the evidence of the miracles"* (John 14:9–11). Many great religious teachers throughout history have taught *about* God. Jesus alone offered proof that he *is* God.

Jesus shows us that *the real God wants us to know him.* That's the irony when we seek to unify the many different man-made pathways towards God. The Lord did not wait for us to find him. He made a beeline towards us by coming into the world as a mortal human being. He endured the squalor of a stable and worked a day job as a carpenter in Nazareth in order to come alongside the people he had created to be his friends. The world religions mark the tracks that have been formed by some of the greatest men and women in their search for God, but Jesus tells us that human searching will always fail at the last. We need God to come and build a pathway for us. Jesus announced that God has done so when he declared that *"I am the Way.... No one comes to the Father except through me"* (John 14:6).

Jesus shows us that *the real God loves us deeply*. Jesus laid his life on the line when he touched lepers. He laid his reputation on the line when he called prostitutes to become his friends. He endured the hatred of his countrymen when he rejected rabbis while accepting repentant Romans and sorrowful Samaritans. When Oprah Winfrey talks about the many different human pathways to what we call God, she misses the point. We can never reach up to God. That's why he has reached down to us.

Jesus shows us that *the real God is holy*. The reason why all of our own man-made pathways to God are doomed to fail is that they fail to grasp how wide the gulf is between us. I can swim much further west off the coast of Cornwall than my three-year-old son, but I am no more able than he is to swim from England to America. The same is true of religious devotion. Some of us are more devout than others, but none of us is devout enough to attain to the completely pure and sinless presence of God. We cannot lift ourselves up to God by our own bootstraps. We need a Saviour who will build a way for us and empower us to travel along it. Jesus has created that God-given highway. His cross has bridged the great divide. That's why he is so honest with us that the real God is far too pure and holy for our own tainted pathways ever to reach him.

Jesus shows us that *the real God is serious*. If God were less holy or more reachable by human endeavours, Jesus would have baulked at dying on the cross. If God were less loving, Jesus would have retaliated against his crucifiers. Instead, he continued his road building as he died, crying out, *"Father, forgive them"* (Luke 23:34).

Jesus also shows us that *the real God will accept anyone*. Before his crucifixion he warned that *"All who have come before me are thieves and robbers"*, so he demonstrated that his new pathway was open to anyone when he promised the real-life robber dying on the cross next to him that *"Today you will be with me in Paradise"* (John 10:8 and Luke 23:43). If you are reading this chapter as a devout Muslim or Hindu or Buddhist or Jew, Jesus is not trying to push you away. He is inviting you to admit that your own religion has run out of road. It has not delivered what it promised you, but all of those unmet promises will be met in Jesus if you reach out to him like the robber who died by his side.

That's why Jesus is not being intolerant when he tells you that there is only one way to God. The true intolerance comes from those who claim that all religions lead to God. What lies beneath this claim is in fact a belief that *no* religion leads to God. They are all simply constructs of our own imagination and therefore equally worthless. The true voice of tolerance belongs to Jesus: *"**Whoever** believes in the Son has eternal life"* and the natural flipside of this: *"But **whoever** rejects the Son will not see life, for God's wrath remains on them"* (John 3:36).

Be tolerant like Jesus. Express the love of God towards people of any and every religion. But be honest like Jesus too. Tell people that because he loves them, God has come to earth to do what all of our religions fail to do. God has built the only pathway that can ever reach him, and he invites each one of us to travel on the pathway he has made for all humankind.

CHAPTER 13

What Happens to People Who Have Never Heard About Jesus?

Talk about a chain reaction. Each time that Jesus answers one of our big questions, it always seems to provoke another one. It's no wonder that people pummel him with so many questions in the contemporary accounts of his life and teaching.

Jesus responded to our question about God's judgment by telling us that God loves us so much that he sent his Son to suffer in our place so that we can be forgiven. That provoked us to ask how this can truly be the only pathway to forgiveness when we live in such a multifaith world. Jesus responded by telling us that man-made pathways only lead to man-made gods, but that provokes yet another question. How will God judge those who have never had the privilege of hearing about Jesus and his God-given pathway? What was the fate of those who lived before Jesus died? What is the fate of those who die without hearing about Jesus today, either because they live in a far-flung part of the world or because they live in a fast-paced secular city and never find the time to read a book like this one? Broadening the question, what happens to the baby that dies or to the person who is born with such severe brain damage that they cannot understand the message of Jesus?

However pressing we may find this question, let's begin by recognizing that it was even more pressing for first-century Jews. Not only was infant mortality far higher in their day, but theirs was a culture that greatly revered its founding fathers and its great religious heroes. Jesus had to reassure them that the patriarchs Abraham, Isaac and Jacob had received prophetic insight about Jesus and were already in heaven (John 8:56, Luke 16:22–31 and Luke 20:37–38). He had to reassure them that the Law of Moses was full of prophetic insight into his God-given pathway (John 5:46). Many ancient Jews had been saved through their faith as they sacrificed lambs at the Tabernacle and Temple (Luke 24:27 and 24:44). But what about the pagan nations of the world, who lacked even this prophetic insight? What about remote people groups today? Jesus doesn't duck this question. He puts himself right where we want him and gives us a straightforward reply.

First, Jesus tells us that it is for our own good that God has not given us a complete answer to this question. He warns a group of religious leaders that *"God knows your hearts"* (Luke 16:15). He tells another group that *"I know you. I know that you do not have the love of God in your hearts"* (John 5:42). Ponder for a moment what might have happened in the Dark Ages if people had been certain that their children were guaranteed salvation if they died before their third birthday, but uncertain thereafter. Imagine what the Europeans might have done to the Africans and Native Americans if they had been convinced that mass extermination would guarantee their mass salvation. It does not bear thinking about. Jesus knows what he is doing when he says, *"I have much more to say to you [but it is] more than you can now bear"* (John 16:12). It is a mercy that the Bible never fully answers this particular question.

That said, Jesus assures us that we can trust God to judge everybody fairly. Nobody will be condemned for having failed to put their faith in a Saviour about whom they never heard. Jesus warned the towns of Galilee, *"Woe to you, Chorazin! Woe to you, Bethsaida! For if the miracles that were performed in you had been performed in Tyre and Sidon, they would have repented long ago in sackcloth and ashes. But I tell you, **it will be more bearable** for Tyre and Sidon on the day of judgment than for you. And you, Capernaum, will you be lifted to the heavens? No, you will go down to Hades. For if the miracles that were performed in you had been performed in Sodom, it would have remained to this day. But I tell you that **it will be more bearable** for Sodom on the day of judgment than for you"* (Matthew 11:21–24).

Note what Jesus is saying here: the Galileans are far guiltier than the people of Tyre and Sidon and Sodom because they have heard far more about God's pathway to salvation. God will not judge those who have not heard about Jesus as if they have heard. Note, however, that Jesus tells us that the people of Tyre and Sidon and Sodom are nevertheless still guilty. People will be judged for having failed to live up to their own sense of right and wrong, however limited that may be. Sodom was still wicked despite its ignorance, because none of us lives up to the standards of our own consciences, never mind the standards of God's Word.[1] Sin is a fatal disease in every people group, even in those groups that have yet to hear the good news that God has provided a cure for the disease through the death and resurrection of his Son.

If you have lost a young child or if you have a loved one who is severely brain-damaged, you need more of an answer than this. It cannot be enough for you to know that God judges people based on the fact that they have sinned, not based on the fact that they have failed to trust in a Saviour about whom they have not heard. Your question must revolve around the fact that your loved one may be unaware of the concept of sin altogether. Jesus therefore has some good news to share with you. He tells us that the Christian message is far easier to understand and to believe than we give people credit for. God has *"hidden these things from the wise and learned, and revealed them to little children"* (Luke 10:21). Jesus even quotes from a psalm that

1   Romans 2:12 states this clearly: *"All who sin apart from the law will also perish apart from the law, and all who sin under the law will be judged by the law."*

goes on to reassure us that it is just as easy for God to initiate faith in a baby as in a professor of theology: *"You brought me out of the womb; you made me trust in you, even at my mother's breast. From birth I was cast on you; from my mother's womb you have been my God"* (Matthew 27:46 and Psalm 22:9–10).

This very basic faith often comes through the infectious faith of parents and of carers, which is why the gospel writers tell us that Jesus looked at the carers of a severely disabled man and *"When Jesus saw **their** faith, he said to the paralysed man, 'Son, your sins are forgiven'"* (Mark 2:5, Matthew 9:2 and Luke 5:20). If we trust in God ourselves, we can also trust him to impart a basic faith to those we influence who are unable to develop faith of their own: *"Let the little children come to me, and do not hinder them, for the kingdom of heaven belongs to such as these"* (Matthew 19:14, Mark 10:14 and Luke 18:16).

But you and I have heard about Jesus. We cannot hide behind this question. We are not ignorant of the God-given pathway Jesus has made for us. Even the act of reading this book has made you guiltier than you were before you read it, unless you respond to the answers that Jesus gives you. If you have not yet surrendered your life to God and laid hold of Jesus as your Saviour, you are living on a knife edge. You were already in danger of God's judgment for failing to live up to your own moral standards, but reading this book has now amplified that danger. You are now aware that the blood of Jesus holds the only cure for human sin, so don't move on from this chapter until you have acted upon all that you have read and heard. Jesus warns you: *"God did not send his Son into the world to condemn the world, but to save the world through him. Whoever believes in him is not condemned, but whoever does not believe stands condemned already because they have not believed in the name of God's one and only Son"* (John 3:17–18).

Once we have placed our faith in Jesus personally, God invites us to become part of his answer to our own question. He has not told us to stay away from those who have not heard about Jesus' death and resurrection for fear that they might reject the Gospel and therefore lose the safety of their ignorance. On the contrary, he has told us to *"Go into all the world and preach the gospel to all creation. Whoever believes and is baptised will be saved, but whoever does not believe will be condemned"* (Mark 16:15–16). If this particular question is important enough for us to place Jesus where we want him and to demand an answer, it is also important enough for us to place ourselves where Jesus wants us – to accept his calling to become his messengers to sinful people who do not yet know that Jesus is the Saviour that they need.

James Hudson Taylor was one of the greatest Christian missionaries to China at a time when its many millions had not yet heard about the death and resurrection of Jesus. He explained what motivated him to endure harsh deprivation on the mission field, remembering the time, shortly after he arrived in China, when he saw a man fall overboard from a crowded riverboat:

I instantly let down the sail and leapt overboard in the hope of finding him. Unsuccessful, I looked around in agonising suspense, and saw close to me a fishing-boat with a peculiar drag-net furnished with hooks, which I knew would bring him up. "Come!" I cried, as hope revived in my heart. "Come and drag over this spot directly; a man is drowning just here!" "Veh bin" (It is not convenient), was the unfeeling answer. "Don't talk of convenience!" cried I in agony; "a man is drowning, I tell you!" "We are busy fishing," they responded, "and cannot come." "Never mind your fishing," I said, "I will give you more money than many a day's fishing will bring; only come—come at once!" "How much money will you give us?" "We cannot stay to discuss that now! Come, or it will be too late. I will give you five dollars"... "We won't do it for that," replied the men. "Give us twenty dollars, and we will drag." "I do not possess so much: do come quickly, and I will give you all I have!" "How much may that be?" "I don't know exactly, about fourteen dollars."

At last, but even then slowly enough, the boat was paddled over, and the net let down. Less than a minute sufficed to bring up the body of the missing man. The fishermen were clamorous and indignant because their exorbitant demand was delayed while efforts at resuscitation were being made. But all was in vain—life was extinct. To myself this incident was profoundly sad and full of significance, suggesting a far more mournful reality. Were not those fishermen actually guilty of this poor Chinaman's death, in that they had the means of saving him at hand, if they would but have used them? Assuredly they were guilty. And yet, let us pause ere we pronounce judgment against them... Is it so hard-hearted, so wicked a thing to neglect to save the body? Of how much sorer punishment, then, is he worthy who leaves the soul to perish?... The Lord Jesus commands, commands me, commands you, my brother, and you, my sister. "Go," says He, "go ye into all the world, and preach the Gospel to every creature." Shall we say to Him, "No, it is not convenient"?[2]

---

2   Hudson Taylor recalled this tragic event in his autobiography, *A Retrospect* (1894).

CHAPTER 14

How Do I Know All This is True?

On one occasion the Jewish rabbis got Jesus right where they wanted him. They cornered him and asked him to prove that everything he taught was true. What miracle would he perform that would signify beyond all doubt that he was truly the Son of God, the only Saviour of the world, the one to whom they must surrender their entire lives?

> He answered, "A wicked and adulterous generation asks for a sign! But none will be given it except the sign of the prophet Jonah. For as Jonah was three days and three nights in the belly of a huge fish, so the Son of Man will be three days and three nights in the heart of the earth. The men of Nineveh will stand up at the judgment with this generation and condemn it; for they repented at the preaching of Jonah, and now something greater than Jonah is here." (Matthew 12:39–41)

I find the way that Jesus answers the Jewish rabbis astonishing. I love the way in which he refuses to dance to their tune. Most of us expect Jesus to act like an insecure teenager at a college party – desperate to impress us with his answers and nervous that we might turn down the chance to follow him. We treat Jesus like a contestant on the TV show *Dragons' Den*, crossing our arms and warning him that if we don't like his answers then we are out.[1] But Jesus evidently doesn't feel that we are doing him a favour by deciding to believe in him. He is the Saviour, not us. He does all the favours. He refuses to perform miracles on demand.

Jesus tells the rabbis that he will only perform one miracle to prove that everything he says is true. Even as he describes it, we can tell that it is a miracle designed to offend people as well as to woo them. He likens his death, burial and resurrection to the Old Testament story of Jonah being swallowed by a giant sea creature and, after spending three days in its belly, being vomited out onto the shore. This is surely one of the hardest Old Testament stories to believe, but that's precisely why Jesus chooses it. He isn't after our reluctant agreement, just so long as his teaching makes sense to our modern ears. He is after our unconditional surrender. He wants to bring us to a place where we confess that everything he says is entirely true, however hard we may find it to believe.

When Jesus died on the cross, it fulfilled several aims. Not only did it mean that he had placed himself right where we wanted him as Saviour, but it also meant that he had placed himself right where we

---

1   For American readers, this is the British version of the TV show you know as *Shark Tank*.

wanted him as the Ultimate Proof-Giver. Jesus saw his death and burial as the equivalent of the moment when Jonah disappeared beneath the waves. As Jesus' corpse was taken down from the cross and buried in a tomb, everyone could see that his life was finished. Only God could save him now.

The Jewish rabbis and their Roman allies took no chances with his corpse. Large crowds of people had been listening when Jesus prophesied about the Sign of Jonah. They therefore sealed the only entrance to the tomb with a two-ton stone, which would require several men to roll it away, and they secured it with a special Roman seal made of clay (Matthew 27:57–66). They posted several armed guards around the tomb, yet on the third day the Sign of Jonah was fulfilled. The stone was rolled away from the tomb, the petrified guards claimed that they saw an angel, and the corpse of Jesus was nowhere to be seen. His followers started declaring that they had seen him raised to life again.

One of the most interesting books about the resurrection of Jesus was written by the Oxford professor Géza Vermes. As a Hungarian Jew who survived the Holocaust, he is quite hostile towards Christianity, yet he admits that the historicity of the empty tomb is undeniable: *"When every argument has been considered and weighed, the only conclusion acceptable to the historian must be that the opinions of the orthodox, the liberal sympathiser and the critical agnostic alike – and even perhaps of the disciples themselves – are simply interpretations of the one disconcerting fact: namely that the women who set out to pay their last respects to Jesus found to their consternation, not a body, but an empty tomb."*[2] Vermes therefore sets out to find an alternative explanation to that of resurrection.

Géza Vermes examines the six best explanations for the empty tomb. Was the body removed in error by the gardener? Was it stolen by the disciples or by someone else as a deliberate act of deception? Not when armed guards were in place to prevent those very things from happening. Besides, the disciples lost their lives rather than deny that they had seen Jesus alive again. Vermes concludes that these three explanations are far harder to reconcile with the facts than resurrection.

In that case, did the women who discovered the empty tomb go to the wrong place? The Jews and Romans would have simply pointed to the right tomb and quashed the resurrection rumours in an instant. Christianity spread like wildfire because the sceptical crowds knew that they had been unable to quash the rumours. In that case, was Jesus buried semi-conscious but still alive, reviving later and rolling away the two-ton stone in order to escape and convince his followers that he was the risen Son of God? Were the reports of Jesus' resurrection simply figments of the overactive imagination of his followers? Vermes concludes that they were far too widespread, far too detailed and far too well corroborated by the empty tomb for any of these alternative theories to be true.

2   Géza Vermes in his book *Jesus the Jew: A Historian's Reading of the Gospels* (1973).

Vermes concludes that *"All in all, none of the six suggested theories stands up to stringent scrutiny."*[3] But then he does something that reveals his personal aversion to the Gospel. Instead of ending his book by concluding that the Sign of Jonah has been fulfilled and that Jesus has indeed been raised from the dead as the ultimate proof that everything he says is true, Vermes starts to grasp at straws. *"Is there another way out of this conundrum that may offer an explanation, if not for the physical resurrection of Jesus, at least for the birth and survival of Christianity?"* The Oxford professor has just refuted every explanation for the empty tomb of Jesus except for resurrection, but then he refuses to believe his own research. He insists that there must be a perfectly rational explanation – it's just that he can't think of one right now. It's an appalling example of what Abraham says to the rich man in the parable we looked at earlier: *"If they do not listen to Moses and the Prophets, they will not be convinced even if someone rises from the dead"* (Luke 16:31).

Jesus has given us all the proof we need to know for sure that everything he says is true. As you near the end of this short book, the issue at stake is not whether Jesus has fully answered all your questions. What is at stake is whether you are willing to be as honest with him as he has been with you. Will you act like the Jewish rabbis, aware deep down that Jesus has fulfilled the Sign of Jonah but unwilling to admit

---

3   Géza Vermes in an expanded version of this section of his earlier book, in *The Resurrection* (2008).

it, clinging onto an alternative explanation you know cannot be true (Matthew 28:1–15)? Will you act like Géza Vermes, following the evidence where it leads until the very moment when your search strikes gold and you begin to discover the big answer to all your questions? Will you shrug off the evidence and simply insist that resurrections do not happen (Acts 26:8–29)? Or will you act like Sherlock Holmes in Sir Arthur Conan Doyle's stories when he tells a client that *"It is an old maxim of mine that when you have excluded the impossible, whatever remains, however improbable, must be the truth"*?[4]

We have almost reached the end of this short book. We have reached the moment of decision. Jesus has given us enough proof that what he says is true for us to be in grave danger of God's judgment unless we confess our sin and ask God to forgive us through the innocent blood Jesus shed for us on the cross. We have reached the moment when each of us needs to pray and tell the Lord that we renounce the self-centred lifestyle of our age and that we surrender ourselves completely to his rule. It is time for us to tell Jesus that we are his servants and that he is our Master. What decision will you make as you finish this chapter? Will you accept the Sign of Jonah?

Who will you trust to define truth for you? Will you trust in politicians and in newspaper editors, whose view of what is true changes from one month

4   He says this in Sir Arthur Conan Doyle's short story *The Adventure of the Beryl Coronet* (1892).

to the other, depending on the changing winds of popular opinion? Will you trust in schoolteachers and in television presenters, even though you know that they will one day die and remain dead? Will you trust in Muhammad, even though he never claimed to have the answers to your questions, confessing freely that he is as much a sinner as we are and that *"I am nothing new among the prophets; I do not know what will happen to me and to my followers; I am only a plain warner"* (Qur'an 46:9 and 48:2).

Will you trust in the Buddha, who died of dysentery after eating an infected piece of pork, and who was cremated in India because everybody knew he was a human who had no power over the grave? Or will you listen to Jesus, who died and was buried and three days later rose from the dead in order to prove to you that everything he says is true?

The Cambridge professor C. F. D. Moule points out that what happened at the first Easter weekend *"rips a great hole in history, a hole the size and shape of the Resurrection."*[5] Jesus has given you plenty of proof. The question is whether you are willing to accept it. How will you respond to his great Sign of Jonah?

---

5   C. F. D. Moule in *The Phenomenon of the New Testament* (1967).

CHAPTER 15

I'm Very Happy in Life – Why Do I Need Jesus?

On the evening of 6th October 539 BC, King Belshazzar of Babylon was partying with his friends. It was a Babylonian national holiday and he was not about to allow the Persian army camped outside the city walls to dampen his exuberant mood. Everybody knew that Babylon was an impregnable fortress city. Even King Cyrus of Persia had been forced to admit that *"I am unable to see how any enemy can take walls of such strength and height by assault."*[1] Belshazzar therefore invited his friends to a party in his palace. Despite the army camped outside, it still felt pretty good to be the king.

But Belshazzar would not have felt so good had he known what was happening just outside his city. The Persian army had spent the past few weeks building makeshift dams in order to divert the River Euphrates away from Babylon. As darkness fell and the sound of celebration filled the night sky, the Persian general

1   The ancient Greek historian Xenophon records these words in his book *Cyropaedia* (7.5.7).

commanded his men to activate the dams. Slowly the riverbed emptied, exposing two broad and undefended channels underneath the mighty walls. By the time King Belshazzar and his party guests realized that the Persian soldiers had managed to tunnel their way into the city, it was too late. Babylon, the most populous, most powerful and most secure city in the world, had fallen. Xenophon tells us that the Persian soldiers *"fell upon them as they were drinking by a blazing fire, and without waiting they dealt with them as with foes."*[2]

Hold that thought. We are acting like King Belshazzar of Babylon whenever we ask this final question: *I'm very happy in life – why do I need Jesus?* Whenever we say this, we are acting as though our lives will go on forever, even though we all know deep down that this simply isn't true. We may have a few more years of life left in us than our parents, but none of us has life in infinite supply. We are all going to die. Denying this and living for the moment makes about as much sense as King Belshazzar sending out party invitations on the eve of the Fall of Babylon.

Whenever we ask this question it betrays a lack of understanding about life and death, but it also betrays a lack of understanding about ourselves. It reveals that we have not yet grasped that the heart of the human problem is the problem of the human heart. All of us are sinners because we all like to act as if we were little kings and queens. We live as if the world revolved

2   Xenophon in *Cyropaedia* (7.5.27). The Fall of Babylon is also described by Herodotus in *Histories* (1.191.1–6) and by the Old Testament in Daniel 5.

around us. Even when we hear the news that Jesus is the true King of the Universe, we instinctively ask how this news will improve the little kingdom we have created for ourselves. We fail to grasp that we live in a universe that revolves around its Creator God and that we are in grave danger because of our attempts to usurp his throne. Judgment Day will come upon us suddenly, just as it came upon ancient Babylon. No matter how happy our lives may be now, we are living on borrowed time.

When Jesus started preaching in Galilee, he therefore did not ask the crowds to let him become their life coach so that he could make them happier. He did not fill his preaching with offers to cure people's loneliness or to make them feel more loved than they did by their boyfriend or their girlfriend. He simply commanded the crowds to *"Repent, for the kingdom of heaven has come near"* (Matthew 4:17). Jesus is the King of Heaven and we are not. It isn't a question of happiness. It is a question of authority.

Jesus is therefore pleased that we have asked this final question. It reveals how much we think like little kings and queens. We are like Prince John at the end of a Robin Hood movie, playacting as the rightful rulers of our little worlds and on the brink of a terrible wake-up call when the rightful Ruler of the world appears. The biggest question in our lives is not whether we will find brief happiness in our daily lives. It is whether we will respond to Jesus as the King of kings and whether we will know true happiness with him throughout eternity.

Jesus expects the fact that he is King to be good news for us. He describes his message as *"the good news of the kingdom of God"* (Luke 4:43). Everywhere we look we can see the foul results of our failed attempts to play at being little rulers of the world, so it is fantastic news that King Jesus has finally stepped in to take over. *"Jesus went through all the towns and villages... proclaiming the good news of the kingdom and healing every disease and sickness"* (Matthew 9:35). Look at the messed-up world all around you. We are in desperate need of the good news of Jesus' Kingdom.

Jesus expects us to view the fact that he is King as such good news that we are willing to give up everything in order to enter into his Kingdom. He told two parables: *"The kingdom of heaven is like treasure hidden in a field. When a man found it, he hid it again, and then in his joy went and sold all he had and bought that field. Again, the kingdom of heaven is like a merchant looking for fine pearls. When he found one of great value, he went away and sold everything he had and bought it"* (Matthew 13:44–46). Those two parables are primarily about Jesus. Because he loves us, he gave up all he had in order to build a pathway for us to enter into his Kingdom. He gave his very lifeblood so that you and I might be spared from the great Judgment Day and admitted to the Paradise he will recreate on earth forever when he has dealt with all the evil in the world. But these two parables are also a call for us to respond with gratitude to this great news. Surrendering to Jesus as your King will cost you everything. There is no such thing as cut-price salvation. It cost him everything he had and it will cost us everything we have to receive it.

Jesus expects the fact that he is King to provoke a crisis in our hearts. This is the hardest decision we ever make in life because it is by far the most important. That's why Jesus warns us not to attempt to negotiate our own terms: *"Not everyone who says to me, 'Lord, Lord,' will enter the kingdom of heaven, but only the one who does the will of my Father who is in heaven"* (Matthew 7:21). It's why Jesus warns the halfhearted that *"you will certainly not enter the kingdom of heaven"* (Matthew 5:20), and it's why he warns the proud that *"unless you change and become like little children, you will never enter the kingdom of heaven"* (Matthew 18:3). It is why he warns those who are happy without him, *"How hard it is for the rich to enter the kingdom of God!"* (Mark 10:23). If surrendering your life to King Jesus seems very costly to you, that's good news. It means that you have understood what surrendering your life to him really means.

But here's the irony: those who refuse Jesus' call to surrender their lives to him only harm themselves. They don't get happier because they decide to continue to act as little kings and queens. They declare war on King Jesus and they choose the path that leads towards eternal misery. They reject the Paradise that could be theirs and they choose to side with Satan and his defeated team of tired rebels on Judgment Day. They don't get happier. They reject the Gospel invitation:

"The thief comes only to steal and kill and destroy; I have come that they may have life, and have it to the full" (John 10:10). As you end this short book, therefore, don't fall for the Devil's bait. He wants to entertain you while he robs you and destroys you. Surrender your life to King Jesus, however costly it appears, because it is the path to true contentment and fulfilment.

Don't cling so hard to your possessions. Jesus tells you, *"Do not worry, saying, 'What shall we eat?' or 'What shall we drink?' or 'What shall we wear?' For the pagans run after all these things, and your heavenly Father knows that you need them. But seek first his kingdom and his righteousness, and all these things will be given to you as well"* (Matthew 6:31–33).

Don't cling so hard to your family and your friends. Jesus gives you a great promise: *"Truly I tell you, no one who has left home or wife or brothers or sisters or parents or children for the sake of the kingdom of God will fail to receive many times as much in this age, and in the age to come eternal life"* (Luke 18:29–30).

Instead, cling to Jesus as your King. Tell him that you have sinned by acting like the little ruler of your own life and that you need to find forgiveness through his death on the cross. Tell him that you believe that God is just. He will not punish your sin twice. Because he punished Jesus in your place, you can be forgiven completely. Then commit yourself to living the rest of your life for Jesus as your King.

As you do so, Jesus promises to come and live inside you through his Holy Spirit. He promises to establish his Kingdom in your heart and to change you from the inside out, making you a messenger to others about the good news of his Kingdom. He promises that people will begin to notice that *"the kingdom of God is within you"* (Luke 17:21).

Throughout this book, Jesus has put himself right where you want him. He has answered your fifteen biggest questions. Now he asks you to put yourself right where he wants you and to answer him just one question: *Will you surrender to me as your King?*

Jesus encourages you as you end this short book, just as he encouraged his original twelve followers:

> *"Whoever wants to save their life will lose it, but whoever loses their life for me and for the gospel will save it. What good is it for someone to gain the whole world, yet forfeit their soul? Or what can anyone give in exchange for their soul? If anyone is ashamed of me and my words in this adulterous and sinful generation, the Son of Man will be ashamed of them when he comes in his Father's glory with the holy angels."* (Mark 8:35–38)

CONCLUSION:
Right Where Jesus Wants You

In April 30 AD, the Roman governor of Judea had Jesus right where he wanted him. Pontius Pilate looked at Jesus standing in his courtroom and began to interrogate his prisoner. He was in charge. He could ask Jesus any question that he wanted. We can read about their conversation in Luke 23:3–4 and in John 18:33–38.

"Pilate asked Jesus, 'Are you the king of the Jews?'" In other words, did Jesus really mean it when he talked about the seriousness of sin and about the terrible reality of Judgment Day? Was he being serious when he warned people that they needed to surrender their lives to him as King?

"'Is that your own idea,' Jesus asked, 'or did others talk to you about me?'" In other words, did Pilate really want to know the answer to his question or was he simply going through the motions in order to appease the Jewish rabbis? *"'Am I a Jew?' Pilate replied."* Not everybody who wants Jesus to sit down and answer

their big questions is willing to sit down and consider his replies.

> *"Jesus said, 'My kingdom is not of this world. If it were, my servants would fight to prevent my arrest by the Jews. But now my kingdom is from another place.' 'You are a king, then!' said Pilate. Jesus answered, 'You are right in saying I am a king. In fact, for this reason I was born, and for this I came into the world, to testify to the truth. Everyone on the side of truth listens to me.'"*

This was Pontius Pilate's big moment. He had heard Jesus' answers to his questions. Jesus had placed himself right where Pilate wanted him. The question now was whether Pilate would be as honest with Jesus as Jesus had been with him. Was he willing to place himself right where Jesus wanted him? Was he willing to accept the truth that Jesus is the Son of God and to surrender to him as the King of the Universe?

"'What is truth?' retorted Pilate. With this he went out again." His dismissive response to Jesus was so tragic that the seventeenth-century philosopher Francis Bacon used it in 1625 in his famous "Essay on Truth" as a prime example of our intellectual dishonesty. Bacon comments: *"'What is truth?' said jesting Pilate, and would not stay for an answer."* As you finish this short book, the same spotlight turns onto you. How will you respond to Jesus' answers? Will you put yourself right where Jesus wants you, or will you simply put this book to one side and walk away?

We put ourselves where Jesus wants us by *confessing our sin*, by admitting that we have lived our lives as if we were little kings or gods. We have tried to make the universe revolve around us and so the Gospel calls us to a Copernican Revolution. Are you ready to confess to God how much your self-centredness has displeased him and how much your life needs to take its proper orbit around his Son?

We put ourselves where Jesus wants us by *trusting in the blood of Jesus for forgiveness*. Regretting our past actions is not the same thing as repenting. Despairing of our sinfulness is not the same thing as having faith in the power of Jesus' blood to grant us forgiveness. We put ourselves where Jesus wants us by believing that he has put himself where we need him. He has endured Judgment Day on our behalf. He really meant it when he told us that *"This is my blood of the covenant, which is poured out for many for the forgiveness of sins"* (Matthew 26:28). Will you be a Pilate or a Peter? Will you be a Judas or a John? Only you can decide.

We put ourselves where Jesus wants us by *surrendering to Jesus as our King*, by vacating our man-made thrones and beginning to live for the glory of God. This will affect the way we behave, the way we spend our time and money, and the goals we set for each day of our lives. One of the first concrete steps of obedience is getting baptized in water, since one of Jesus' first commands is, *"Whoever believes and is baptised will be saved, but whoever does not believe will be condemned"* (Mark 16:16). In Christian baptism, a new believer goes underwater to express the fact that they have died to their old way of living. They come up out of the water to express the fact that they have begun a new life in Jesus, marching to the beat of his drum and obeying his commands every day. If you want to follow Jesus then baptism needs to be at the top of your new list of things to do.

You may find it helpful to watch four short videos I have produced for new believers in Jesus. You can access them for free at **www.everyday.org.uk/ new**. You may also find it helpful to watch some of the messages I have preached to the church I lead in London about what following Jesus each day means in terms of money, sex, forgiving others and pouring out your life to help those around you. You can find these free videos at **www.everyday.org.uk/sermons**. Ultimately, you need to find your own church where other people in your own neighbourhood can help you to grow as a follower of Jesus. If you are prayerful and persistent, God will help you to find the right church for you. Throughout the Bible, Jesus describes the Church as his beloved Bride, and he promises to help you to love the Church as much as he does.

Finally, making Jesus your King means reading the Bible every day to see how he wants to guide you. Start by reading a chapter of Matthew's gospel each day. This will enable God to guide you very clearly in your first month of following Jesus. When you finish Matthew, turn to John's gospel and enjoy the perspective of a different disciple, then turn to the book of Acts to see how the earliest believers worked out their faith in Jesus every day. To help you in this, I have written a series of devotional commentaries on the Bible in a similar style to *Jesus, Right Where You Want Him*. If you have enjoyed this little book, you will find these commentaries very helpful, explaining to you what each chapter of the Bible says and challenging you to face up to what that means. You can find all of the books in the *Straight to the Heart* series of commentaries through any good book retailer or by visiting **www.philmoorebooks.com**.

But enough about these extra resources. For now, it is decision time. Jesus has placed himself right where you want him. As you finish this book, he calls you to place yourself where he wants you too. My prayer is that you will end this short book by praying to King Jesus. Tell him that you are ready to follow him every day, as he continues to give you honest answers to your big questions.

GAGGING JESUS

Things Jesus Said We Wish He Hadn't

Phil Moore

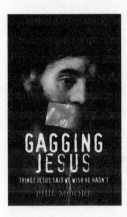

"Whether you are a believer or merely a curious sceptic, this book will help you to discover Jesus as he really is."
Sandy Millar, co-founder of the Alpha Course

Jesus of Nazareth wasn't afraid to tell it like it is. Those who claim to follow him, on the other hand, often are.

It's easy to settle for a tamed and domesticated Jesus. A bound-and-gagged Jesus. A Jesus of our own thinking. That's why this book focuses on the fifteen most outrageous things Jesus said: the fifteen things you are least likely to hear preached about in church.

If you ever suspected that Jesus wasn't crucified for acting like a polite vicar in a pair of socks and sandals, then this book is for you. Fasten your seatbelt and get ready to discover the real Jesus in all his outrageous, ungagged glory.

"Downright dangerous! It demands attention. Prepare to be shocked, undone, and put back together again."
Greg Haslam, Senior Pastor, Westminster Chapel, London, UK

ISBN 978 0 85721 453 9 | £4.99 | $7.99

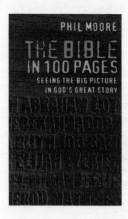

THE BIBLE IN 100 PAGES

Seeing the Big Picture in God's Great Story

Phil Moore

"If you want to get a grip on the Bible, this is a great place to start."
R. T. Kendall, theologian and author of *Sermon on the Mount*

Most people want to discover the message of the Bible. The problem is simply that they are too busy. It just looks far too long. When they do read it, they often find it hard to see the wood for the trees amongst its 66 books, 1,189 chapters and 31,102 verses. That's why *The Bible in 100 Pages* is so important. It will help you to see the big picture in God's great story. It will help you to read the Bible with fresh eyes.

"Bold, fresh, fast-moving, relevant and often controversial, The Bible in 100 Pages *gives you the best of Phil Moore, and the best of the Bible. An excellent resource for anyone wanting to get their heads round the biblical story."*
Andrew Wilson, author of *If God, Then What?*

ISBN 978 0 85721 551 2 | £4.99 | $7.99

STRAIGHT TO THE HEART SERIES
TITLES AVAILABLE: OLD TESTAMENT

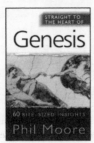

ISBN 978 0 85721 001 2

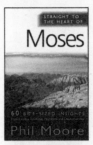

ISBN 978 0 85721 056 2

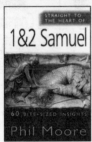

ISBN 978 0 85721 252 8

ISBN 978 0 85721 428 7

ISBN 978 0 85721 426 3

STRAIGHT TO THE HEART SERIES

TITLES AVAILABLE: NEW TESTAMENT

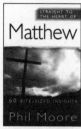

ISBN 978 1 85424 988 3

ISBN 978 0 85721 642 7

ISBN 978 0 85721 253 5

ISBN 978 1 85424 989 0

ISBN 978 0 85721 057 9

ISBN 978 0 85721 002 9

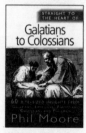

ISBN 978 0 85721 546 8

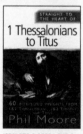

ISBN 978 0 85721 548 2

ISBN 978 0 85721 668 7

ISBN 978 1 85424 990 6